Routledge Library Editions

LAMENT FOR ECONOMICS

ECONOMICS

Routledge Library Editions – Economics

METHODOLOGY & PHILOSOPHY OF ECONOMICS
In 5 Volumes

I	Economics and Economic Policy in Britain, 1946-1966	*Hutchison*
II	'Positive' Economics and Policy Objectives	*Hutchison*
III	Economics and Sociology	*Löwe*
IV	Economic Doctrine and Method	*Schumpeter*
V	Lament for Economics	*Wootton*

LAMENT FOR ECONOMICS

BARBARA WOOTTON

Routledge
Taylor & Francis Group
LONDON AND NEW YORK

First published in 1938

Reprinted in 2003 by
Routledge
2 Park Square, Milton Park, Abingdon, Oxon, OX14 4RN
or
270 Madison Avenue, New York, NY 10016

First issued in paperback 2010

Routledge is an imprint of the Taylor & Francis Group

British Library Cataloguing in Publication Data
A CIP catalogue record for this book
is available from the British Library

Lament for Economics
ISBN 978-0-415-31390-2 (hbk)
ISBN 978-0-415-60800-8 (pbk)
ISBN 978-0-415-31385-8 (set)

Miniset: Methodology & Philosophy of Economics

Series: Routledge Library Editions – Economics

LAMENT FOR ECONOMICS

by

BARBARA WOOTTON

Routledge
Taylor & Francis Group
LONDON AND NEW YORK

FIRST PUBLISHED IN 1938

"The age of chivalry is gone: that of sophisters, economists and calculators has succeeded: and the glory of Europe is extinguished for ever."

EDMUND BURKE, 1790

"Equilibrium is just equilibrium."

PROFESSOR LIONEL ROBBINS, 1932

PREFACE

THIS is not a work of research. "Pre-research" would be a more appropriate word, and would better serve to emphasize the essentially preparatory nature of all that I have attempted. That the uneasiness to which I have sought to give expression in these pages is both widespread and well-founded I am certain: and equally certain that it obtains amongst many whose intelligence and sense of social responsibility forbids that their opinion should be lightly dismissed. Whether I have succeeded in representing—or have only distorted—the views of this public, it is for others to judge. I can, however, claim to have tried very hard myself to practise the principles which I have preached on pp. 309–313 of this book. The inadequacy of such constructive proposals as have resulted from this attempt is, I know, only too conspicuous; but if my critics will also accept the rule that to criticize is to incur an obligation to search for a remedy, something of value may eventually result even from this vague and sketchy outline.

Most of my many obligations must, I fear, of necessity remain unacknowledged. It would however be very ungracious not to mention how much I owe to a great and miscellaneous company of non-professional students. In social studies the men and women who think with their feet on the ground, and who continually refer the results of their own and others' thought to the touchstone of experience in the workaday world, have a specially valuable contribution to make. My friends and helpers in that public, too numerous to be individually named, will, I hope, accept this generalized expression of an indebtedness which it is difficult to overestimate.

Nor can I let pass this opportunity of expressing my gratitude to two sources from which I have derived continual inspiration and encouragement. The masterly sanity that pervades the writings of Mr. H. G. Wells has probably done more than anything else to keep alive in myself (as in how many others?) belief in the potentialities of applying intelligence to the solution of the problems of social life; while the explosive genius of Professor Lancelot Hogben has been a continual stimulus to fight the temptations of inertia and slovenly thinking. I need only add that neither of these thinkers has the slightest responsibility for anything that appears in these pages; and that one, if not both, of them would probably be astonished to find himself mentioned here.

B. W.

LONDON
September 1937

CONTENTS

LAMENT FOR ECONOMICS

CHAPTER I

THE INDICTMENT

I

THE present plight of economic studies is both distressing and paradoxical. On the one hand, the preoccupation of the world at large with what are commonly regarded as economic problems—that is to say questions of work and wages, of trade and markets, of tariffs and currencies—has perhaps never been so great as it is to-day. It is these topics which crowd the pages of electoral programmes or make ceaseless claims upon the attention of dictators. Indeed, to-day, you cannot be in any real sense a citizen unless you are also in some degree an economist; and it is becoming the practice to explain all manner of phenomena in economic terms, even including many that do not, on the face of them, look economic at all. When the spokesmen of governments trot out the old phraseology about prestige or national honour, the modern fashion is to regard these as just diplomatic synonyms for commercial competition or the struggle for markets; and there are even those who assert that *all* the happenings of political or social life take the form that they do, and no other, on account of some overmastering "economic necessity" in the background. Wars, it is said, are begun and ended, governments come and go, ideologies and "-isms" have their day of favour—all because the iron laws of economics will not have it otherwise.

That is one side of the picture. And, from looking at this alone, one would not unreasonably infer that the professional economists of the day would be among the most influential, and most highly-respected, of all the men of learning; whereas, in actual fact, there can seldom have been an age in which the public at large placed a lower estimate on the usefulness of professional students of economics. Indeed, the economist is rapidly becoming the stock butt for popular jest. "All the economists in the world if put end to end would not reach . . . a conclusion." "Wherever six economists are gathered there are seven opinions, and two of them are Mr. . . . 's"; and so on.

It is, therefore, hardly surprising to find that the economist, in face of this urgent demand for his services, and general contempt for them when received, should suffer from what has been aptly described as an "agonizing sense of shame."[1] It is, no doubt, one variety of some such emotion that prompts the writing of this essay, as it has prompted also

[1] Robinson, *Economics of Imperfect Competition*, p. 2.

the noticeably increasing output of works upon the methodology of economics, or of economic apologias of one sort or another. For the dilemma is not easy to ignore. Either the traditional lines of contemporary economic thinking are destined to perpetual sterility, or they are not. If they are, then no time should be lost in scrapping the present apparatus and giving our whole energies to the search for some more promising approach. But if, on the contrary, the situation is not so bad as this, it would still be, at the least, good policy on the part of the economists to explain as best they can why progress is not more conspicuous than it is; and why the common man's anticipations of what economic studies ought to be able to achieve are so frequently doomed to disappointment.

II

It may be useful at the outset to draw up a kind of charge sheet, listing the principal accusations which are to-day laid at the door of the economists.

First and foremost is the charge that economics is *no use.* In effect this complaint really covers all the more specific charges set out below, since the latter do but offer possible explanations of the alleged futility of current economic theories. It is, therefore, necessary to point out straight away that those who belittle the economists for their uselessness concede by implication that it is their business to be useful. Hence those who do not accept this implication are under no obligation to defend themselves on this particular count, and can to that extent afford to adopt an attitude of lordly indifference to their detractors. A certain proportion of the professional economists of to-day are, I suspect, prepared to adopt this attitude, and to rank themselves amongst those pure scientists who, engaged in extending the boundaries of knowledge, have no concern whatever with the possible utility of their discoveries from any point of view. The propriety, or impropriety, of this attitude can, I think, hardly be established by intellectual argument. Whether an economist (or any other student, for that matter) ought to aim at some usefulness, other than that of establishing facts or truths that were not previously known, is a question of ultimates. Everyone must make up his own mind about it in the light of his own particular system of values. I cannot therefore do more than simply register the statement that I for one do not believe that the study of economics should be undertaken in a spirit of indifference to its practical utility as a means of improving the conditions of human life. Once this is said we shall all fall out again, of course, over what is meant by "improving" conditions. These difficulties can, however, be left in the background for the present, since our only purpose at the moment is to separate those who believe that the economist ought to try to contribute to "improvement" (in whatever sense) from those who take the opposite view; and to warn the latter that, since the whole of this essay is written upon an assumption that they do not share, all that follows will be irrelevance to them.

As soon as this declaration of faith has been made, it will probably be well to state quite precisely what it does *not* mean. It does not, for example, mean that every line of enquiry from which no practically valuable result has emerged ought to be forthwith abandoned. If that were so, no research would indeed ever be begun at all; since, at the moment at which it is initiated, no enquiry can possibly have already yielded fruitful results. The earliest stages must always be barren; hence, if that which is barren is to be immediately discontinued, nothing will ever be done at all. What is meant is, rather, that so long as nothing of practical utility emerges, the student will feel his task to be unfulfilled; and in choosing which of several alternative lines of enquiry he shall follow, he will be guided by his estimate of the prospective utility of additional knowledge in various fields. He will, in fact, attempt to enlarge the range of economic knowledge and understanding at just those points where he believes that our present ignorance is most harmful. It will be less personal curiosity, than a guess at what will be fruitful in a practical sense, that will dictate the course of his researches.

Again, the view that it is the ultimate purpose of economic studies to "do good" casts no reflection upon those students who claim no more than an indirect utility for their work. Professor Pigou's distinction, as elaborated by Mrs. Robinson,[1] between the "tool-makers" and the "tool-users," is illuminating in this connection. The man who makes a spade does not, directly, feed anybody; but his reason for making a spade is, none the less, that he expects it to contribute indirectly to that end, through the help which it will give to the farmer who is actually and directly engaged in the production of food. In just the same way the (relatively) pure economist, faced with the charge that he is no use, can, with Mrs. Robinson, beg his accusers to have patience while he perfects his tools "in the hope of being able sooner or later to meet the practical man's requirements." But the admission of this hope at once classes him with those who share that conception of the ultimate objective of economic studies which I have postulated in this essay.

Subject, then, only to these safeguards, the economist who admits an obligation to be directly or indirectly useful cannot blandly dismiss as irrelevant the charge that he fails in this respect. He must, on the contrary, go on to consider the more specific forms in which this accusation is framed.

[1] *Economics of Imperfect Competition*, pp. 1, 2.

III

Here the first charge to be faced is that current economics is unintelligible to the plain man. What is the use, it is asked, of a whole system of abracadabra which has no meaning except to the initiated? Once upon a time professors of economics wrote the masterly English prose of Adam Smith or John Stuart Mill. Now their pages are spattered with complicated diagrams, technical mathematical symbols, or, at the best, arguments so abstruse and so abstract that only those generally familiar with their tortuous courses can hope to follow them at all. The plain man, and still more the plain politician, looking to the economist for help in solving concrete economic problems, concludes despairingly that, since the economists are incapable of speaking any language that he can understand, their services are not for him.

Now by itself this would, of course, not matter at all. Nobody quarrels with the physicists or the chemists because those not versed in these subjects cannot understand the Proceedings of the Royal Society. On the contrary, the layman is apt indeed to revere the man of science the more for the very technicality and abstruseness of his writings and processes. And the economist may retort that there is no reason why the man in the street should expect to find the *Economic Journal* easier reading than say the *Journal of the*

Chemical Society; while at the same time he silences possible dissension in his own ranks by biting references to writers "unacquainted with" a certain tool "who resent its use by others."[1]

This, however, is not quite the whole story. For this is just what the economist cannot afford to ignore —that people who meekly accept the unintelligibility of many sciences become resentful when the same quality is exhibited in treatises on economics. There must be a reason for such discrimination. Two possible alternatives here present themselves. The first is that economics being a very young "science" is only just reaching the stage at which the use of a specialized technique becomes fruitful. All science is merely the elaboration of ordinary people's reflections about various aspects of the universe. It begins with such simple observations and crude hypotheses as are within the competence of any intelligent man, and only becomes the province of the expert, when the refinements of process, and the volume of material already accumulated, have developed so far as to call for an equipment beyond that provided by an ordinary "general" education. Economics, it may be argued, is just now arriving at this stage. If we want it to be as fruitful as other sciences have become, we must not grudge it the use of those very methods, with all their technicality, that have given such astonishingly fertile

[1] Pigou, Preface to *The Theory of Unemployment.*

results in other spheres. But in this case it is intelligible that the plain man, who now for the first time finds himself warned off the field as no longer competent to take part in economic discussions, does not find it easy to appreciate the new situation.

The merits of this particular plea need not detain us at the moment. Here we are only concerned to make clear that *some* reason must be found to explain why the technicality of economic studies should commonly be regarded as a sign of their futility, while the use of a much more elaborate technique in chemistry or medical research is regarded rather as a sign of the potential fruitfulness of these branches of science.

The second likely cause for such discrimination seems to be that the public does not accept the implied analogy between economics and other sciences. If the economist could deliver the kind of results that the chemist, the doctor or the physicist delivers, then, says the public, we would recognize both his title to rank as a Man of Science and our own incapacity to understand, or to criticize, the processes by which his results are achieved. But we are not prepared to let him have it both ways—to admit his claim to be master of the secret mysteries of science, and yet to forego all those magnificent achievements which the Men of Science have taught us to expect from their work.

This line of argument clearly raises large issues as to the place and purpose of economic studies, and it is accordingly discussed at length in what follows.[1] In the meantime, if the persistence of this attack leads economists to eschew unnecessary obscurity, and to take all the pains that they can to express in readily intelligible terms whatever can be so expressed without loss of accuracy, no harm will have been done. There is no merit in technicality for technicality's sake. Nor is it amiss at times to recall the late Professor Cannan's reminder that "most of the simplest things in economics have never been put in such a way as to carry conviction to the mind of the sort of person who is in the great majority of every public"; and that "the blame is not altogether to be put on his feeble mind, but in large measure on the unnecessarily complicated expositions offered by the economists."[2]

IV

Next comes the charge that the economists cannot agree. This, perhaps, is the loudest and most frequent complaint of all. Before, however, the defendants begin to prepare their case in reply to it, they may legitimately ask that the exact meaning of the accusation should be stated as precisely as possible. Does it, for example, mean that there is no agreed body of doctrine,

[1] See below, pp. 111 ff.

[2] "The Need for Simpler Economics," *Economic Journal*, vol. xliii, No. 171.

no series of propositions which command the general consent of professional economists, and which neither have to be established afresh, nor are liable to refutation, by every newcomer to the subject—nothing, in fact, which has the status enjoyed by an elementary textbook of chemistry or physiology? Or is the ground of complaint, rather, that no two economists can be relied upon to give the same advice in any concrete situation?

If the first of these interpretations is correct, the economist can put up quite a good case without much difficulty. While there are differences of opinion about refinements and incidentals, there remains a core of economic analysis the correctness of which is not now disputed within the ranks of economists themselves. As I write this, I realize, however, that the critic may well reply that this is no defence at all, since most economists would exclude from their definition of an economist all those who did not accept these very doctrines. To say that a group of people are agreed about certain things is mere tautology when such agreement is a necessary condition of being admitted to the group at all. And point is certainly given to this countercharge when we find, for example, Mr. Erich Roll (who as B.Com., Ph.D. and Head of the Department of Economics in the University College of Hull presumably would claim to be an economist) quoting an opinion of Professor J. W. Scott (Professor of

Logic and Philosophy at University College, Cardiff) with which he does not agree, and at the same time attempting to remove the damaging effect that the sight of these dissensions might have upon the reader's mind by appending in a footnote the categorical statement that: "Professor Scott, it should be noted, is not an economist."[1] In the absence of any agreed definition of the term "economist" the possibility of such charges and countercharges is, I fear, quite inevitable. The only logical attitude would seem to be to define "economists" as those who hold accredited positions for study and research in economics (which, in effect, means those who are appointed to University or similar posts as teachers or research workers in that subject); and to point out that the man in the street cannot have it both ways. He cannot *both* claim the right to say who are, and who are not, to rank as economists, *and* complain that those whose credentials he, and he alone, has approved, fail to subscribe to the same doctrine. While, admittedly, it may be true that economists, within the terms of my definition, agree about certain things because they would not hold their jobs unless they did, at least that does not alter the fact that, if for this or any other reason they *do* so agree, they are at least so far exempt from blame on the score of disagreement! And there is this also to be said in support of the—as may be thought slightly cynical—definition of an

[1] Roll, *About Money*, p. 108.

economist as a person who can get somebody to employ him in that capacity, that it does seem to be largely against such "official" economists that complaint is directed. Even such public as has meekly accepted the view that, for example, Mr. John Strachey or Major Douglas or Professor Soddy have no more status as "economists" than has Professor Pigou as a politician, Mr. Keynes as an engineer, or I myself as a physicist—even this public still complains that there is no unity of doctrine within the innermost priesthood itself.

Now if, as was suggested just now, this charge is to be taken literally to cover the whole body of economic theory, then, we may repeat, it certainly is not true. The main outlines of what is sometimes shortly described as "marginalism" or, alternatively, as "equilibrium economics," and the analysis, in terms of this theory, of movements of demand, supply and price in markets of all kinds—labour markets, capital markets, money markets, markets for consumption goods, and the rest of them—here is a *corpus* of doctrine, the validity of which, within its own assumptions, would hardly be denied by any professional economists. True, there are plenty of unresolved difficulties, even on the theoretical plane. Trade cycle theory, to take the most conspicuous contemporary example, is still a field in which no orthodoxy can claim to have convincingly established its rights to rule. But no one need be disturbed by that, any more than by the parallel disagreement amongst doctors as to the causation of cancer. Such controversies in territory that is as yet unconquered in no way damage the security of the conquests that have already been made. Without disagreements at the circumference no science can hope to make advances: without agreement at the centre there is no science at all. And certainly, in the field of theory at least, the economists have their agreements as well as their divergences. Nor is it they who are to blame if the public insists on concentrating attention upon the one to the exclusion of the other. Any economist could mention off-hand half a dozen textbooks, the reputability of which would be admitted by any of his colleagues. To this extent the charge that there are as many varieties of economics as there are economists is plainly based on ignorance.

In practice, of course, those who are disposed to ridicule the conflict of opinion amongst economists are not concerned with theory at all. The real gravamen of this charge lies in its alternative form—in the suggestion that economists of the most impeccable standing offer opposing counsels in exactly the same circumstances. Some say deflate, some devaluate: some that employment would be greater if wages were reduced, others that to increase employment wages should be kept up and the rate of interest brought down; and so on and so forth. Even the least economically learned reader of these pages will be able to furnish only too many examples for himself. Nor can the economists excuse themselves entirely by taking up the attitude that it is not their business to say what "ought" to be done, on the ground that this depends upon views of the ultimate nature of the Good Society, or the Good Life, upon which they are no better qualified to speak than anybody else. Faced with the demand that he should indicate how this country may be made fit for heroes to live in, an economist might indeed retort that he has no way of judging what sort of conditions are specially appropriate to a race of heroes. Should there be hardship and difficulty, such as will give room for display of the heroic virtues? Should there be economic equality, or is one hero to be preferred in rank and wealth to another? Most contemporary economists would modestly disclaim any special ability to pronounce upon such large issues as these.

But no such plea will serve in the many cases in which such fundamentals are not involved at all; in which it is a question, not of building some Utopia in England's grey and smoky land, but of judging policies in the light of their power to promote such specific ends as, say, an increase in the volume of employment. From the point of view of this one objective alone, at this one particular date, what advice have the economists to offer? Should we raise the tariff or lower it? Restore the gold standard? Practise public economy or spend lavishly on public works? If the economists cannot give consistent answers to such questions as these, what, asks the despairing public—what on earth *can* they do? That their answers should be cautious and guarded, hedged about with safeguarding "ifs" and "buts"—that we could understand and forgive. After all, we know well enough that there are few simple roads to anywhere that can be safely followed, without question, in all circumstances. It is a general rule that the way to extinguish a fire is to throw water upon it; but we do not think the worse of those who have enunciated this rule for pointing out that it is not applicable in cases where the fire is caused by burning petrol or the water is drawn from the sea. But what contempt should we not feel for the chemists, if half of them told us that the way to put out a fire is to pour water upon it, while the other half recommended douching it with paraffin? And this, it is widely, and not unjustifiably, felt, is just the sort of advice that the economists give.

To this line of attack the economist who takes his obligations seriously, and does sincerely believe that it is his duty to be useful, is extremely sensitive. His most natural line of defence is, no doubt, to beg the practical man, in the terms quoted above from Mrs. Robinson,[1] to have patience while he perfects his tools.

[1] See p. 18.

But at the same time it will not come amiss if the clamour of the mob outside the gates impels him once again to look over the design of those tools, in the light of the purposes which they are intended ultimately to serve. For nothing can prevent the labour of the most conscientious and skilful tool-maker from being wasted, if the process for which his tools are appropriate should become obsolete. Certainly, no economist can fail to see the significance of the contrast between the public's indifference to the—quite respectably substantial—volume of accepted economic theory, and its acute awareness of the diversity of learned economic opinion upon concrete issues. He cannot shut his eyes to the fact that outside (to say nothing of inside) the ranks of the professional economists the greatest scepticism prevails as to the whole relationship between current economic theory and the solution of practical economic problems. Already there are too many who have approached the serious study of economic theory with high expectations of its practical fruitfulness, only to abandon this, sooner or later, with a great sense of disillusion. It is possible, of course, to reprimand all these, on the lines already indicated, for their impatience, and to reiterate that if they would but persevere a little longer, they would ultimately perceive the bearing of theoretical studies upon practical problems. If any one chooses to make this rebuke, it is indeed impossible to prove him *wrong*. But at the same time it is reasonable to ask the economic theorists at least to show that they have some apparently probable ground for thinking that their present abstractions will eventually ripen into something of concrete and practical utility. Nor should it be forgotten that here too the study of economics may be in a different position from many of the natural sciences. For even assuming (what I for one would not be prepared to admit) that the same obligation lies on, say, the physicist, as on the economist, to achieve results that will "do good," the former is, as we have just seen, comparatively untroubled by insinuations that there is little connection between the mysterious processes of his laboratory and the workaday life of the public outside. For the efficiency of those processes is sufficiently attested by the continued and plainly visible stream of inventions which does in fact emerge from the labours of the scientific investigators. It is on this account that the layman neither expects to *understand* the learned pronouncements of the Men of Science, nor feels called upon to *question their values* from his own point of view. Here and there the spokesmen of the business world may indeed express dissatisfaction with the "results," in a commercial sense, of the scientific workers whom they themselves employ. But, in so doing, they certainly do not speak for any widely-felt distrust of the fertility of current methods of research. Those who have visibly changed the face of the world have nothing to fear from complaints that they set about doing this, in the first instance, by means of a technique which seems to the uninitiated to have singularly little relation to any familiar "reality." It is only when an apparently unreal technique continues barren of "real" results that suspicion begins to be aroused.[1]

V

Thus, in effect, a further charge emerges—namely, that the economists ignore reality. It has already been suggested that they show a lamentable ineptitude, if and when they do condescend to notice the complex world in which we actually live, in making useful, or indeed even consistent, propositions, about it; and the reason for this, it is now added, is that they have spent too much time in minute examination of a form of society which does not exist outside the sphere of their own, rather quaint, imaginations. The study of imaginary worlds which are conceived in some detail may certainly call for the exercise of much ingenuity. The nursery poet, for example, who wrote:

> If all the world were apple-pie
> And all the sea were ink,
> And all the trees were bread and cheese
> What should we do for drink?

[1] For further discussion of this whole topic, see below, pp. 116 ff.

certainly posed a problem to which it is not easy to give a ready and satisfactory answer. Yet no University Chairs have been founded for the study of this particular group of problems, although these would unquestionably become of the gravest importance, should the conditions postulated in the first three lines of the poem be realized. And the simple reason is, first, that nobody has the slightest grounds for supposing that the world is likely to turn into apple-pie, the sea into ink, or trees into bread and cheese; and, second, that there is also no reason to suppose that this strange poetic fancy is linked with the prosaic world of common experience in any way which would make the study of the one likely to throw light upon the workings of the other.

But the economists, it is murmured on all hands, seem to have settled down quite complacently to exhaustive analysis of a world hardly less fantastic than that pictured by our poet; and here, it is suggested, lies a simple and convincing explanation of their deplorable imperfections in the rôle of either prophet or doctor in actual situations.

In the chapter which immediately follows, the validity of the accusation that contemporary economic theory has no contact with reality is discussed in some detail. Here it may be useful to note that, for the sake of simplicity and brevity, the term "apple-pie world" will be borrowed from our nursery poet, and used throughout this essay to describe conditions so far removed from anything in current experience as to give no reasonable ground for hope that, by their analysis, the phenomena of ordinary life may be usefully elucidated.

VI

Finally, the economists have to face the fact that they are widely suspected of being somehow in league with the powers of darkness, or at least of not being as disinterested as they should be. All their elaborate theories are, it is said, at bottom just a system of apologetics for the particular economic system under which we of Western Europe and North America are now living; or, if not exactly for this system, at least for one which approximates to it pretty closely. Under pretence of impartial diagnosis and scientific study they are insiduously advocating biassed policies. Here indeed, the economists can at least congratulate themselves that this accusation is hardly compatible with the previous charge that they never concern themselves with reality at all. Even the greatest subtlety will hardly make a man an effective propagandist for something the existence of which he has never realized. But this does not mean more than that the economists are relieved of the necessity of defending themselves against this charge only in the unhappy event of their being found guilty under that which precedes it.

And there is, in addition, a postscript to this allegation of bias. For if economic theory is just a system of apologetics for a particular mode of managing economic affairs (generally described as "capitalism"), then it would have no relevance to a world which went about things differently. In particular, the economists could have nothing to contribute towards the solution of the problems of a socialist society. They would have to confine themselves to pointing out that a socialist form of organization is pernicious in comparison with that to which their theories relate. It is thus in a double sense that the economists are suspected of being the mouthpieces of the powers that be—on the one hand, in the rôle of explicit or implicit defenders of things as they are; and, on the other hand, in the sense that their teachings are meaningless, and that they have, therefore, nothing to offer, to any economic organization substantially different from that under which the modern Western European or the American goes about his daily business.

VII

Such, then, are the main heads of the indictment. It may be that there are items which I have omitted. Be this as it may, the list is formidable enough as it stands.

The economic theory of to-day, it is alleged, is useless because it is unintelligible; because, after all their arduous studies, the economists cannot be relied upon not to give diametrically opposite diagnoses and prognoses of the same situation (not to mention the incompatibility of the various remedies which a few of the more courageous among them are sometimes induced to prescribe); because the economists feed on their own tails by busying themselves with the analysis of imaginary worlds which they have themselves invented; and finally because they are passing off as the result of purely scientific enquiry what is in reality no more than a partisan advocacy of particular social policies.

It has already been suggested that the charge of unintelligibility would by itself carry no weight, and that it would indeed never have arisen, except in conjunction with the others. This charge, accordingly, will not be pursued further. In an attempt to estimate the force of the remaining counts in the indictment, I propose, in the first place, to discuss the relation between the content of contemporary economic theory and the realities of the plain man's experience. This will lead to consideration of the why and the wherefore of those fallibilities and disharmonies, which make the public treat the statements of even the most reputable economists with a disrespect which they would never dream of showing before the accredited professors of any of the natural sciences. This in turn will involve some discussion of the whole basis of the claim of current economic theory to rank as a "science." Next I shall take up the charge that economics is merely apologetics, and meaningless except in relation to the particular conditions for which it is said to serve as an apology. This will include some enquiry into the validity of the alleged apologies. In conclusion, I shall try to indicate along what lines the economics of the future must develop, if it is hereafter to be proof against such of the criticisms listed above as may turn out to be well-founded.

CHAPTER 2

THE RELATION OF ECONOMIC THEORY TO THE ACTUAL ECONOMIC WORLD

I

IT is not easy to find a satisfactory short definition of the substantial content of traditional English economic theory. On the whole the most useful formula seems to be that which defines economic theory as *the study of market processes*—useful, that is, in the sense that it is both handy and accurate, and does actually describe the territory that the economists claim as their peculiar province. By market processes I mean the mutual interactions, in any sphere, of demand, supply and price (or value). The exact limitations of the concept of the market are discussed more fully below.[1] For the moment I propose to take for granted that the reader, at least in the light of the examples that follow, will have a reasonably clear idea of what is meant.

A simple test of the appropriateness of this definition is to consider what would remain of current economic literature if the basic assumptions of the market were, so to speak, ruled out of order. The whole theory of values and the concept of equilibrium, in the first place,

[1] See Chapter 5.

as elaborated (to go no further back) by Marshall or Wicksteed[1] is patently a theory of market movements. It is concerned with discussion of what would happen to the price or value of something should there be changes in the supply of, or demand for, it; or conversely of what would be the effects of changes in supply or demand upon price. "Equilibrium" is a concept of such central importance that modern economic theory is often simply designated "equilibrium economics," equilibrium meaning the equilibration of these very market forces of demand, supply and price, which is attained when the price of x is such that the quantity of x demanded at that price will be equal to the quantity of it offered for sale at that price. If there were no such processes as demanding, selling and pricing, clearly this statement could have no meaning.

Now since this equilibrium-value business is, in its various forms, the stock-pattern key used by the economists to unlock the door to every theoretical problem, it follows that the inferences and propositions that they make in their more specialized enquiries are equally dependent upon this postulate of market pro-

[1] The reader who does not already have a fairly clear idea of what economics is all about should read any simple book of economic theory—such as Clay's *Economics for the General Reader*, or Cunnison's *Economics*, or Scott's *Approach to Economics* (if he does not wish to go too far into subtleties); or (if he is prepared for something a little more arduous) Wicksteed's *Common Sense of Political Economy*, vol. i, or Marshall's *Principles of Economics*.

cedures. Consider, for example, theories of the distribution of income; or the theories of money or of the incidence and effects of taxation and other forms of Government interference; or the vast literature on the subject of investment, saving and cycles of prosperity and depression. Each of these discussions is conducted in the framework of its appropriate market or markets. Thus, if there were no labour market, if, that is to say, some people did not seek to sell their labour and others to buy it, the bottom would drop out of propositions about what would "happen" to the rate of wages, or the supply of labour, in this field or that, should such and such a line of Trade Union policy be adopted, or this or that invention introduced. Without the concept of a labour market Mr. Hicks, for example, could never have written his subtle (and depressing) *Theory of Wages*, nor indeed could anybody else have made any other theories on that subject in his place. So also if there were no capital, investment or property markets, if business did not consist of buying (or demanding) goods, of pricing and selling (or supplying) them, there would be no theories of profits, interest or rent. And by the same token, if we had no markets, monetary theory, which is concerned with analysis of the mutual interactions of demand, supply and prices in many fields, would likewise be annihilated. Such propositions as that an increase or decrease in the supply of currency or means of payment will tend to cause such and such changes in the prices of commodities, in the incomes of such and such groups, or in the relative production of capital as compared with consumption goods would become meaningless. In every case the link between cause and effect is forged in some market or other. The influence of an increase in the supply of means of payment upon the production of capital goods is established through the changes which it effects upon people's readiness to buy and sell these goods, as expressed in the market for them; and the tendency of such an increase to cause a general rise in prices is simply due to the effect upon market conditions of the fact that it puts more money into the hands of many buyers. Similarly the—often quite exceptionally subtle—analysis of the far-reaching effects of the imposition of a tax upon some commodity is simply a matter of charting the consequences of this measure in every market that may conceivably be affected by it. A tax on tea, for example, tends to raise the price of tea owing to its effects in the market for that commodity itself. But since tea is a staple national beverage, all who have to pay more for their tea now find that their incomes no longer go so far as they did; and this in turn may affect their willingness to sell their labour, or the use of their property, at the same price as formerly; and so on.[1] And to take up the

[1] The reader who is interested to see to what lengths this particular type of analysis can be carried should read some such text

final example suggested above, analysis of the possible causes of cyclical movements of prosperity, as evolved by Professor Pigou,[1] Professor Hayek,[2] or Mr. Keynes[3] is fundamentally a matter of disentangling the mutual interactions of events in many related markets—notably the investment market, the money market, the market for consumption goods and the labour market.

II

The reader who has even a cursory acquaintance with economic literature will not, I think, easily dispute that English classical economics is essentially the study of the procedures of the market-place, including in this term, of course, the many cases in which the word "place" is purely figurative, the market having no tangible geographical home. Before, however, we consider more precisely the implications of the conception of a market, it may be useful to tie up the definition of economic theory here put forward with two others that have an established title to respect.

First is the late Professor Marshall's long-famous definition of economics as the "study of mankind in

on problems of incidence as Professor Seligman's *Incidence of Taxation*; or if he wishes to confine himself strictly to *English* thought, Mr. Silverman's *Taxation: Its Incidence and Effects.*

[1] E.g. *Industrial Fluctuations.*

[2] E.g. *Prices and Production.*

[3] E.g. *The General Theory of Employment, Interest and Money.*

the ordinary business of life" examining "that part of individual and social action which is most closely connected with the attainment and with the use of the material requisites of wellbeing."[1] Now this, it is immediately evident, is a definition which is capable of covering a great deal more than the phenomena of markets, or of what is sometimes called the market economy. Robinson Crusoe (whose adventures would very likely by now have passed completely into oblivion had it not been for the affection of the economists for him) never went to market; but he certainly engaged in action "closely connected with the attainment and with the use of the material requisites of wellbeing." Moreover, quite apart from Crusoe and others in his position, such a definition might easily cover the study of many phenomena which affect people who do go to market, but which are not themselves reflected in any market movements; or it might comprise study of market phenomena, from some aspect other than that of the effects which these phenomena may produce in this or that market. For instance, in the attainment of "the material requisite of wellbeing" known as coal, workers often become afflicted with the disease known as nystagmus. Conceivably, the chances of contracting this disease are amongst the influences which affect the supply of labour in coal-mining, the wages of coal-miners and the price of coal,

[1] *Principles of Economics*, 6th edition, p. 1.

and are accordingly responsible for certain reactions in these markets; but, be this as it may, Professor Marshall's definition would enable enquiries into the purely medical aspects of nystagmus, or into any psychological effects that it may have upon its victims or their families, to pass under the guise of economic studies. Or to take a less extreme example, an analysis of the structure of Trade Unions or of Joint Stock Companies, Cooperative Societies or municipal enterprises, from the point of view of their administrative structure or of their competence in a purely legal sense, might reasonably pass as part of the "study of mankind in the ordinary business of life." It is true, of course, that all the institutions named do, in fact, engage in market activities; but that does not mean that there is not abundant material in them for study quite apart from any effect which they may have upon the demand, supply or price of anything.

Moreover, no one can deny that the attainment of the material requisites of wellbeing can hardly be successfully pursued unless we have some conception of what those requisites are; which in turn might reasonably be held to imply that we must also have a clear picture of the nature of wellbeing itself. In this way the boundaries of economic studies as plotted by Marshall might be found to include discussions of the nature of human needs, physiological and psychological, not to mention also philosophical speculations as to the meaning of wellbeing; whilst under the heading of the "use of the material requisites of wellbeing" a place might properly be found for studies of practically the whole range of human activity viewed from almost any conceivable angle—aesthetic, biological, psychological or what-not; for it is hardly possible to "do" anything, without incidentally using some of the material requisites of wellbeing in the course of whatever is done. On this basis a study of a football match from the point of view of the technical competence of the players as footballers would be quite relevant; for a football match requires the use of such important material requisites as land, timber, leather and various textiles. It only touches the world of markets in respect of such matters as the wages paid to the players or the "gate" which the match realizes: but many an elaborate analysis of matches can be, and is, made, in which these issues are but minor incidentals, if indeed they appear at all.

At the moment I am not concerned with the advantages or disadvantages of permitting the economists to roam in the very wide fields which such a definition as Marshall's would assign as their rightful kingdom. As we shall see later, they may do better with too much freedom than with too little.[1] At this stage it is only necessary to note that Marshall's vision of the range of economic studies was, potentially at least, much

[1] See below, pp. 266 ff.

wider than that permitted by any definition in terms of markets.

This point would be of greater importance if, in fact, any actual body of recognized economic doctrine had yet been built upon anything like the whole reach of Marshall's very extensive foundations; for then it would be quite unfair to discuss the whole achievement of economic theory in terms of that part of it which alone happened to be concerned with market processes. Actually, of course, nothing of the kind has happened. Economic studies, as commonly so called, have consisted, on the one hand, of the formulation of a body of economic laws or propositions which relate strictly to market processes of one kind or another; and on the other hand of a mass of "realistic" or "institutional studies" which pass as economics (if indeed they are permitted so to pass at all) solely because the particular institutions or activities of which they treat have had some special importance in determining the concrete background in which, at particular times or places, the laws of the market have in fact operated. Under the one head we have all the propositions that claim to rank as economic laws, or to constitute the "science" of economics; while under the other head studies of Trade Unions, or of systems of land tenure, or of municipal tramways struggle uneasily for recognition, along with such researches into industrial fatigue or accidents as are not solely medical.

I say "struggle uneasily" because, Marshall's definition being loose enough to include any and every kind of humanistic study, the limits to which it may in practice be extended have become virtually a matter of convention.

More recently, greater precision has been given to the scope of economics by defining this as the study of the "forms assumed by human behaviour in disposing of scarce means" between alternative uses.[1] This is at once more comprehensive and more restricted than the Marshallian view of the economist's business. It is more comprehensive, since it draws no line between the "material" and the "non-material" requisites for the attainment of wellbeing, and so evades the awkward philosophic problems which arise when the question is put whether Marshall's definition would permit a study of the principles determining the incomes paid to clergymen to pass as economics or not. On the other hand, the Robbinsian definition is more restricted, since if the economist is to consider only how scarce means may be distributed between alternative uses, it follows that he is only interested in institutional studies in so far as these throw light upon how this is, has been, or may be, done.

Now, clearly, it is possible to dispose scarce means between alternative uses without recourse to any market. As Professor Robbins has himself pointed

[1] Robbins, *Nature and Significance of Economic Science*, p. 15.

out,[1] Crusoe had to distribute his time between many needs that clamoured for satisfaction; and a closed communistic society, which did not use money or markets at all, would have to distribute its resources somehow or other between the claims of all its members for the satisfaction of all their needs. But, as Professor Robbins is again the first to admit, although both Crusoe and the wholly communistic society would be faced with these problems and would presumably solve them somehow, that is all that can be said on the matter, within the terms of his definition. Crusoe and the communists would do—whatever they decided to do, and that is the end of it. There are no "interesting complications,"[2] or, if there are, they are completely intractable by any discipline which would subsume them under an orderly series of laws or propositions. It is true that the time and materials which Crusoe spends in building a house cannot also be employed in catching fish, and that the labour and resources which the leaders of a communistic society assign to the making of cosmetics cannot also be used for baking cakes. It is also true that if Crusoe or the communist leaders wish that they had paid more attention to fish and cakes, and less to houses and cosmetics respectively, we can point out to them that they have not made their scarce means go so far in fulfilling their alternative uses as they might; but they will hardly

[1] Op. cit., p. 18.

[2] Op. cit., p. 20.

thank us for the information; and we are dependent for our ability to go even this far upon their own statement of their own judgment of what they would have preferred to do.. Obviously there is no material here which would justify the establishment of University chairs in economics.

The potential significance, for the whole future of economic studies, of this intimate connection between the modern conception of economics and the exchange or market economy can hardly escape the reader's notice. It is discussed at length below. For the moment, however, I am only concerned to establish that a definition of economics as the study of market activities is in harmony with the Robbinsian view of the subject as the study of the disposal of scarce means between alternative uses. It can, I think, claim to be a fair description of that hard core of economic theory which is covered both by Marshall's and by Robbins's definition, and which is, in fact, the main preoccupation of whose who to-day are responsible for the formal teaching of the subject in schools and universities.

III

Now if any substantial (not to mention useful) body of theory is to be built up about market processes, it is apparent that those processes must have a certain *objectivity*. If the interconnections between supply, demand and price are subject to someone's arbitrary caprice, then again there is nothing more to be said about them. The phenomena of the market will then be whatever that someone decides that they shall be; whereas all phenomena that are amenable to generalization, or can be built into any coherent theory must, so to speak, enjoy a certain independence of status.

That market phenomena are commonly accredited with this status is shown by the very language in which they are described. We speak of rising or falling prices, increasing or diminishing demand or supply, just as we speak of rising or falling temperatures, or the increasing or diminishing incidence of certain diseases, and this in spite of the fact that everybody knows that the prices of goods, or the quantity of them which is produced or sold, is in the last resort entirely a matter of human volition. If there are changes in these various quantities, these occur because somebody somewhere has decided to alter them. A chart of price movements may look very like a temperature chart, and may even be studied by much the same technique; but this cannot alter the fact that no man can make the sun shine more or less warmly; whereas price tickets bear figures that human beings have decided that they shall bear, and are themselves affixed by human hands.

In assuming, therefore, that market phenomena have an objectivity comparable to that of natural occurrences, the economist is postulating that the acts of will to which changes in the market are immediately traceable will themselves show a certain uniformity. The manager who gives instructions that all goods shall be marked down by a certain percentage on the opening day of his Winter Sale, and subsequently modifies these figures as the Sale proceeds, is not doing this just for fun or to gratify some caprice. He is presumed to have his reasons, and it is further presumed that *these reasons are not peculiar* to him; that they would *in general* actuate you or me in the same way if we were placed in the same circumstances; though, since no two of us would read those circumstances in exactly the same way, it is not to be expected that our course would coincide exactly with his.

The economist's market, real or imaginary, therefore, rests upon certain assumptions about human behaviour, all of which are implied every time that he makes even such a simple statement as that herrings are cheap when they are plentiful. These assumptions are familiar enough to any who have even a superficial acquaintance with economic theory; and they need, therefore, only be stated quite briefly here. The most important is the assumption that, in their market activities, people will attempt to behave economically, that is to say, that in their disposal of scarce means between alternative uses they will do their best to make the means go as far as possible in fulfilment of the said uses. This assumption is basic, in the sense that the economist begins by analysis of a completely perfect market, a kind of Platonic Idea of a market, in which all movements are the outcome of behaviour of this kind. Having thus satisfied himself as to what would happen if everybody always did behave like this, he then goes on to modify and elaborate his theory to meet the cases in which people do not, or might not, conform to this pattern. The important point is that these adulterations of pure theory, no matter how numerous they may be, or how extensive their influence, must always be treated as departures from a norm; for it is the existence of this norm which alone gives any kind of coherent unity to the whole discussion. And it follows that in applying his theory to any concrete situation, the economist will proceed by way of assuming that everybody's behaviour is throughout governed by the principle of economy as stated above, except when reasons are specifically given for thinking that this assumption is not valid. Taking for granted that we all invest our capital in the most profitable investment that we know, the economist may stop to explain why, on occasion, some of us do not do this but never vice versâ.

Now the assumption that market processes result from a particular mode of behaviour implies, of course, that it is *possible* for people to behave in that way. If such behaviour is not even possible, economics must be written down at once as concerned only with what in the preceding chapter was labelled an "apple-pie" world. In practice this platitude is significant for two reasons. The first is that the whole conception of a market is bound up with such institutions as the law of property, and the right of freedom of contract, more or less in the form in which these obtain in contemporary England or America. One cannot dispose one's scarce means economically between competing uses, if one is not permitted by law to have any means, or if having them does not include any right of deciding what to do with them. Of course this does not mean that *unrestricted* rights of property and *unrestricted* contractual freedom are necessary assumptions of all economics. It simply means that these rights, like the principle of economic behaviour, are assumed to be present except when they are explicitly excluded.

Further, a theory of market processes implies that there must be, so to speak, some common language of the market-place, in terms of which people can make their behaviour intelligible to other people, so that one can react upon another. And this language must also serve the economist when he seeks to compound a number of market phenomena under one generalization. In practice this means that the market economy must also be a money economy.[1] Theoretically, indeed,

[1] The converse proposition—that a money economy must also be a market economy—does not, of course, follow; since money

all the operations of pricing (in the sense of valuing things in terms of other things), buying and selling can be conducted without the use of any common monetary measure. We can all quote cases where these operations are actually performed by way of direct barter, either in communities which are too primitive to have yet attempted the use of money, or in those in which the monetary system employed is so inefficient as to be a hindrance rather than a help. But notwithstanding these oddities and fringes, it is hardly necessary to labour the point that a theory of market activities could never, for sheer cumbrousness, develop beyond a most rudimentary stage, if it could not express itself in monetary terms. I only wish to call attention here to the perhaps rather obvious fact that market economy implies a market language, because at a later stage of the argument there will be much to be said about the accuracy of that language as a vehicle for conveying that which is often read into it.[1]

Finally, a study of what happens inside a market is to be differentiated from a study of what happens outside it. That is to say, the economist who takes the market as his province, does not concern himself with the cause of the causes, the market effects of which he attempts to disentangle. A Japanese architect who

values may be placed upon commodities or services by authority, without those values being determined by any objective market process. See below, pp. 294, 245.

[1] See below, pp. 144 ff; 192.

wishes to design an earthquake-proof house does not consider that it is his business to investigate the peculiar formation of the earth's crust which makes his country particularly liable to seismic disturbance. On the contrary, taking the earthquake as his datum, he gives his whole attention to studying the elasticity or power of resistance to shocks, offered by various types of building material or design. So also the market economist does not occupy himself with the why and the wherefore of those patterns of demand, or of those technical conditions of production, which are the ultimate progenitors of all that happens in his market. As Professor Robbins has admirably expressed the matter in the work from which I have already quoted: "Economics is not concerned at all with any ends *as such* . . . It takes the ends as given in scales of relative valuation . . . "; and again: "The technical arts of production are simply to be grouped among the *given* factors influencing the relative scarcity of different economic goods."[1] The demand for aspidistras, that is to say, may diminish owing to the spread of a belief that the presence of an aspidistra is a mark of an inferior social status in a household. All manner of consequences will follow, affecting the price of aspidistras, the incomes of those who grow or import these plants, the demand for the pots in which they are customarily displayed, and so on and so on. With all

[1] *Nature and Significance of Economic Science*, pp. 30, 33.

of these the economist will busy himself, trying to sort them out according to the chart provided by what he calls his theory; but (at least in the Robbinsian view), not his to reason why (or how) such beliefs establish themselves, still less whether people's desire to assert their social superiority over their neighbours is the kind of need which the scarce means of the community may properly be employed to satisfy. And similarly on the side of supply, the orthodox economist will consider the effects upon output and prices of the introduction of a moving conveyor system into a factory, without concerning himself either with the mechanical principle upon which the conveyor operates, or with its effect upon the nervous systems of the operators, the pace of whose work it determines.

IV

This, then, is the field of contemporary economic theory. Basically it is the study of the disposal of scarce means between alternative uses, taking both the means and the uses as ultimate data. But in practice we find that the scope of the study is more closelylimited by the fact that the complex and interesting aspects of this business of economizing are just those which arise in *markets*—that is to say, in conditions where the attempts of independent units to dispose their scarce means economically between the alternatives of their choice are embodied in objective movements of value, demand and supply, as expressed in monetary terms.

The phrase "independent units" in the preceding sentence needs to be circumscribed a little more clearly before we can tackle the job of comparing the economist's hypothetical market with the plain man's experience. For these words carry an aroma of competition. Is it the implication that the economist's analysis is necessarily confined to competitive, as distinct from monopolized, markets? If so, that analysis must necessarily be losing its relevance to a world in which the rapid spread of combinations in restraint of trade has become a commonplace.

Originally, as any student knows, the traditional English value, or equilibrium, theory was a theory of competitive markets. Thirty years ago competition was treated as the norm, and upon this basis the Marshall–Wicksteed structure, which is still the backbone of English economic thought, was erected. The possibility of restriction upon competition was, however, by no means overlooked, and the student who had mastered the interactions of price, demand and supply under competitive conditions would be led on, in a later chapter, to consider what changes in his conclusions he must make, if the sellers (or, more rarely, the buyers), whom he had previously imagined to be acting independently of one another, should all be merged into one entity, or should collectively decide, as a matter of policy, to present a united front towards those to whom they sell, or from whom they buy.

More recently the practice of treating all monopoly problems as aberrations from a normal state of competition has been severely criticized, as illustrative of the economist's alleged blindness to the realities of the world whose workings he is supposed to be elucidating; and, in deference to this criticism, a great deal of attention has lately been paid to the theory of "monopolistic" or imperfect competition.[1] Unfortunately for the economist, this—in itself praiseworthy—attempt to keep economic theory in contact with the facts of experience opens up some rather ominous prospects for the future of that theory, the significance of which is discussed below.[2] For the moment, therefore, I shall revert to the original competitive conception of market processes, and ask what utility this type of analysis (which, notwithstanding the modern developments just mentioned, is still extensively employed) can claim to offer as a key to concrete economic problems.

Now, nobody would, I suppose, deny that very passable likenesses of the economist's markets are to be found in all sorts of places; or that, where these do not already exist, they are often struggling to be born.

[1] Notably in the two path-breaking works: Mrs. Robinson's *Economics of Imperfect Competition*; and Chamberlin's *Theory of Monopolistic Competition*.

[2] See pp. 82 ff.

At the one end of the scale we have the stock and produce markets, conforming almost perfectly to the economist's prototype. In these markets prices have great flexibility, and react most sensitively to every change in the conditions, actual or anticipated, of demand and supply. Those who bid up and down the price of cotton in Liverpool are but the impersonal mechanisms through which the rainfall, the boll-weevil or the policies of the American administration transmit their influence on to the Lancashire manufacturer. These prices are thus "objectively" determined; and the immediate agencies by which this determination is effected are persons whose behaviour is, in this context, reliably acquisitive; persons, that is to say, who follow the prospect of profit as faithfully as a homing pigeon makes for home. There is no caprice here. Hence all the implied generalizations about human behaviour which the economist's laws of demand, supply and price presume, are valid enough in such cases as this. So also in the stock markets. There may indeed be a few puritan or gentle souls who eschew investment in breweries or in armament firms. These delicacies, however, do not trouble the greater part of the investing public; and, since peculiarities of this kind *are* peculiar, and do not reflect any consistent general trend, they can safely be neglected in all propositions about stock market movements, except those which are quantitative. In other words, if there is a preponderant tendency among investors to seek those investments which are most remunerative, the fact that a minority are also influenced by miscellaneous considerations of another kind will not invalidate such statements, as that a rise in the current rate of interest will tend to cause a fall in the value of fixed-interest-bearing securities; just as the practice of public vaccination will tend to diminish the incidence of smallpox even though, on the one hand, there are many unvaccinated persons who may come into contact with the disease and yet remain immune, and on the other hand, there may even be some who are definitely poisoned by the vaccine. In analysing the workings of competitive stock and produce markets no critic, however severe, will seriously suggest that the economist need have qualms lest the *nature* of the links between demand, supply and price should fail to be such as his methods presume.

These characteristic markets, moreover, the economist may plead, are, after all, but the most highly developed forms of that which in a more rudimentary stage is familiar everywhere. That is what is meant by the statement made above that where markets do not exist they are struggling to be born. Take, for example, the labour market. Notwithstanding the declaration (to be found among the many oddities of the Treaty of Versailles) to the effect that the "labour of a human being should not be treated as merchandise or as an article of commerce," the labour of all human beings practically everywhere is directly, or indirectly, treated as merchandise or as an article of commerce.[1] To be sure most labour markets are much less conformable to the ideal of pure theory than are stock and produce exchanges; for they are cluttered up with all sorts of irrelevances like tradition, or parental influence or nepotism, which inhibit the smooth and effective working of market forces. Looking back over the course of our own lives, or of those of our friends, few of us, probably, could confidently assert that our careers into and out of various jobs had followed any principles which would harmonize with any consistent relation between the price and the supply of labour in the various occupations concerned. To most of us obstinacy, stupidity, necessity and luck would appear to have had at least as large a part to play, as any reasonably intelligent pursuit of the principle of economy in the distribution of our labour between the alternative uses (if any) that have been open to it. Certainly the oddities, which we dismissed as negligible in the stock markets, are very much more important here.

Yet when all is said, the "labour market" is a

[1] Even the "plans" of Soviet Russia are fulfilled by workers who sell their labour for wages; and, even there, when a particular type of labour is needed with special urgency, this increased "demand" is often reflected in higher wages.

visible enough reality. The scope of market mechanisms generally must be admitted to be pretty wide. What is there in this world that does not ultimately have its price? And how—outside Soviet Russia, or the domain of the Nazi Price-Controller, or such "interferences" as the Trade Boards of this country—are prices determined except by the changing conditions of demand and supply, as reflected in the attempts of human beings to use their scarce means economically? And what is the result of all this network of moving prices, what in fact are prices *for*, unless it is, in their turn, to influence the supply of, and the demand for, this and that commodity? Every day, before our eyes, this market system opens and closes a thousand fascinating possibilities and moulds the destiny of millions—changing the coffee plantations of Brazil into orange groves, damping out the furnaces of South Wales and Durham, or setting the deft fingers of Japanese children to making paper toys and trinkets. The markets of experience may be imperfect or impure in comparison with those of the textbooks; but one can hardly deny either their existence or their influence upon our lives.

V

So far, so good. But the fact that the economist can bring creditable evidence to show that the ideal markets of the textbooks have their actual counterparts in the familiar world of experience hardly makes it *less* odd that progress in the application of his theory should be so uncertain and so slow.

One important clue to this puzzle reveals itself, I think, so soon as we examine a little more closely what normally happens in these various markets, and what are the relations between them. And here the first thing to be said is that markets are apt to be very active places, and that the relation between the various processes operating in any given market, or between one market and another, are apt to be very complicated relations. Those who recall, for example, the kaleidoscopic changes that took place in the economic picture as the result of the attempt in 1935 of certain Powers to impose sanctions upon Italy in the Abyssinian war will realize how intricate are the interconnections of modern markets. The impoverishment of South Wales miners, or the diversion of the demand for gorgonzola cheese to Danish roquefort, were among the nearer, and more evident, ripples set up by this particular stone.

It is this intricacy in the network of relations between one market and another which is, I suggest, at least in part responsible for the gap between the tool-makers and the tool-users in economic studies, lamented, on behalf of us all, by Mrs. Robinson.[1]

[1] See above, p. 18.

And here too we have, I think, one of the differences which distinguish economic problems from those of a technical, or, in the accepted sense, of a scientific nature. The kind of question in economics to which it is important to get a reasonably reliable answer refuses to be circumscribed within manageable limits. There is no end to it, and still more is there no end to the answer to it. And, unfortunately (to resume the metaphor used above) the ripples which occur farthest away (in time or place or logical connection) from the point where the stone fell into the pond, may be just as important as those near the centre. Technical problems, on the other hand, such as those concerned with the construction and flight of aeroplanes, are problems strictly relating to aeroplanes and the conditions in which they fly. Their business is with the qualities of various materials, with fuels or with wind-resistances, and they do not need to go far beyond such topics; whereas some of the *major* consequences of British currency policy may be found on the rubber plantations of Java or the Silesian coal-fields. The flight of an aeroplane no doubt also sets up a chain of reactions in the environment which is literally unending; but, from the technician's point of view, the remoter links in this chain can generally be dismissed as unimportant, and attention can be concentrated upon a relatively limited field. In other words, technical problems can, at least in a great number of cases, be satisfactorily studied in isolation, and the results of isolated studies can be compounded for practical purposes without material loss of usefulness; whereas the elaborate interconnections of economic problems, and the indivisibility of economic structures, make this isolation of particular problems or factors almost impossible to achieve except at the cost of grave departure from reality. *Abstract* economic analysis, itself, of course, presents no difficulty, as the abundant literature of the subject sufficiently testifies. What is lacking is any effective means of communication between abstract theory and concrete application.

In face of the formidable difficulties offered by this complexity, the analytical economist usually pleads, first and foremost, for more time in which to extend the range of his hypothesis, so that it may cover all the conditions that are relevant to any actual problem that is put to him. Suppose, for example, that he is asked to forecast the results to be anticipated, should the Government decide to embark upon a mildly inflationary policy as from, say, the second week of January 1938. In this case, if his analysis has not gone further than the simple statement that an increase in the means of payment tends to raise the domestic price-level, and to lower the foreign value of the currency affected, it will not be surprising if the inflation produces results which he has not covered by this crude generalization, or even if it perhaps fails to reveal those which he has. If he has been rash enough to communicate so incomplete a theory, and to allow it to be "applied" to this practical problem, he will certainly be discredited.

So in order to avoid this discredit, the economist sets to work to elaborate his analysis, always in terms of those basic market processes which we have found to be the essential instruments of his thought. He now takes into account that the new currency may encounter a variety of obstacles, as it seeps its way through into that stream of effective demand which alone operates directly upon the prices of goods. If obstacles (or rigidities) occur at point (*a*), the flow will be directed in such and such a way; if at point (*b*) it will be directed in this other way; if at point (*c*) . . . and so on up to or beyond (*z*). Moreover, in addition to following this particular chain he must also go back and differentiate between the case (*a*) in which the instruments of production are fully used when the new injection of currency occurred, and (*b*) that in which they are not; and each of these hypotheses will in its turn need subdivision by many others. . . .

The final upshot of the whole business (if indeed there is any finality in the matter at all) is the propagation of a truly monstrous brood of hypotheses such as might well alarm some Malthus of the speculative world. Now, conceivably, in this way a system may be built up which is so complete that it will always somewhere comprise an appropriate hypothesis to cover every situation that may arise. When that day comes, we shall at last be able, by turning up our economic manuals, to find the circumstances in which any given change in the economic situation occurs fully covered by, say, chapter 1, section 2, sub-section (iii), sub-sub-section (*e*). The motorist on the road, whose car stops unexpectedly, refers to what the manufacturers who supply it so disarmingly describe as "a fault-finding table." With the aid of the alternative hypotheses provided by this, he eliminates and eliminates, until he arrives at a series of propositions which exactly fit his case. For example: if the carburettor still floods when the float needle is depressed, he eliminates all the alarming list of possible mishaps which may block the petrol system between tank and carburettor. If when the engine is turned over, there are sparks at the plugs, he clears the ignition of blame; and so on. In similar fashion, the economist might conceivably in the end produce analyses comprehensive enough to be useful.

But I must confess that for my own part I do not feel very hopeful about this prospect—least of all in the light of what the increasing subtlety of economic analysis has to date accomplished. I am all for patient and elaborate speculation in fields where it looks like being fruitful. But the test of fruitfulness must surely be the measure in which the thinker succeeds in delivering interim results as his speculation follows its laborious course. And by this test it seems to me that contemporary economic theorizing fails more often than it succeeds. I know that this is an opinion which must simply rest upon personal judgment of imponderables, and which cannot be established by a mere list of citations. In support of my view I can but plead, first, that I can find very little evidence that the ability of economists to interpret concrete situations usefully has advanced appreciably during the past hundred years; and second, that this sceptical estimate of the fruitfulness of contemporary economic theory is, in my experience, shared by a very considerable proportion of students whose time has been occupied in mastering the latest evolutions of that theory. These manifestations, to quote one of the ablest of such students[1] "remind me of nothing so much as of the strange forms taken by certain reptiles in early geological epochs before they became extinct." In the past few years I have repeatedly heard colleagues who are engaged in adult education in economic subjects assert (and I plead guilty to the same sentiments myself) that they can no longer bring themselves to include any substantial slice of current economic

[1] Mr. H. S. Booker, to whom I am indebted for permission to quote this analogy.

theory in their courses; not because the subject is too difficult, but because it is sterile and unreal, and because, no matter how it is presented, it only provokes ridicule or disgust. Equally has it been my experience to hear from both students and teachers of economics within the gates of more than one University increasingly frequent and emphatic expressions of disillusion and scepticism, resulting from a sense of the futility of the complex trains of thought which the theoretical economists of to-day are pursuing.

This dissatisfaction cannot, I think, be dismissed, as symptomatic merely of unreasonable impatience; and, most emphatically, it cannot be met by substituting crude generalizations for more subtle ones. If the foresaid tools of economic thought are unsatisfactory, nothing but harm can come from using the same tools in a more slovenly way. But, equally, can no good result from the laborious perfecting of tools if these are fundamentally unsuited to the work for which they are intended. If—to drop the metaphor—a particular line of enquiry is slow in yielding results, there is, on the face of it, at least a case for re-examining the initial presumption that it was worth following. Those who are lost in the desert are not entitled to assume, without more ado, that the direction in which they happen to be travelling is the shortest, if not the only, road to safety.

VI

This pessimistic view as to the helplessness of economic analysis in face of the complexity of market phenomena is, moreover, aggravated by one or two other considerations. The economist's appeal to the public and to the politicians to have patience is particularly unfortunate. In too many of the concrete problems of economic life it is impossible to wait till the economist's analysis is complete, since the situations themselves will not wait. And in this connection even what is generally called doing nothing is equivalent to doing one thing in preference to others. Ruritania, perhaps, imposes fresh quotas upon British coal. What kind of readjustments, it is asked, are in consequence to be anticipated in the light of the theory of international trade? To wait for an answer until that theory, with its curves of relative elasticity of demand and so forth, has been elaborated sufficiently to cover all possibilities of this particular case will not be much use, since by that time many of the most important readjustments about which we are specially anxious to be informed will already have occurred. To be sure, the economist can indeed plead that in this respect professors of sciences as respected as that of medicine are sometimes found to be equally as impotent as he, and with no less disastrous results. Cancer victims cannot wait to die until medical research has discovered the cause and cure of their disease. But if the doctors are still baffled by this particular problem they can at least point to a creditable record of achievement in respect of many others. The trouble with the economists is, not so much that their analysis is unripe for practical application just at this or that point, but that their failures are so much more conspicuous than their successes, and that the signs of progress in the practical field are so difficult to distinguish.

And there is worse to come. Suppose that the economist has succeeded in working out some part of his theory to a very creditable degree of completeness and complexity—as for example, the theory of the elasticity of demand. Every first-year student is acquainted with this theory of elasticity of demand and knows the type of conditions which determine its magnitude. Now Professor Robbins has suggested[1] that it would not be a very difficult matter to apply this theory to some actual problem, and to work out, in the light of it, the elasticity of demand for, say, herrings at a given date in all the circumstances of that date. "... computations of this sort," he says, "are not really very difficult and may have considerable utility for certain purposes." This is encouraging; though the encouragement would be greater if the statement were supported by an imposing array of instances in

[1] *Nature and Significance of Economic Science*, p. 108.

which such calculations have in fact been made, and have in fact proved to be of practical utility. (One may indeed hint in passing that the economist's position in the public esteem would be revolutionized if he really did make a practice of embodying such theoretical concepts as elasticity of demand in concrete quantitative terms so accurate, that the business man who habitually took these researches into account in determining his output, price and investment policy habitually beat the business man who would have nothing to do with them. But let that pass). Let us assume that the theory of the elasticity of demand, or some other part of the theoretical economist's apparatus, is *capable* of application to a concrete situation, even if it is not habitually and successfully thus applied.

Now this theory is worked out, as every theory must be, on the assumption that all potentially disturbing factors are safely impounded in the prison of *ceteris paribus*—other things remaining equal. We may follow Professor Robbins whole-heartedly when he explains that an Eat More Herrings campaign (or a fashion for Herring parties among the Younger Set)[1] might so modify the whole demand-schedule for these fish as to render irrelevant (and therefore misleading) a calculation that an x per cent increase in their supply would cause a y per cent fall in their

[1] My example.

price, made prior to the inauguration of this campaign; and that no conclusion can stand up to such changes in its original premises as these. But those who are concerned with the practical value of economic analysis can hardly be content to let the matter rest there. They are bound to ask what are the prospects that *ceteris paribus* will, in the real world, prove to be an effectively guarded prison? In that world it always takes a certain time for effect to follow cause, and how much may not happen in that time! The swollen flood of herrings has to overcome various obstacles on its way to market; the dealer and retailer have both to see and to believe, before the price adjustment takes place; and the public has in its turn to wake up to the fact that herrings are cheap to-day, and to adapt its menus accordingly. In the case of a familiar and highly perishable commodity like herrings these adjustments may indeed be prompt enough; but how far is this case typical? Nobody will, I think, deny that in many of the markets that we know even such primary reactions as the adjustment of price to changes in supply, and of demand to these price changes, take place in very dilatory fashion. The fact is widely recognized, for instance, in many labour markets, and in the markets for goods of quite moderate durability. And, moreover, even where the immediate reactions to some change in market conditions make themselves apparent quite promptly, there are almost sure to be secondary consequences, the full realization of which takes some considerable time. Changes in the price of herrings will in their turn affect the price of bacon, or the demand for cornflakes or other breakfast foods. Nor (as has already been suggested) is there any reason to suppose that secondary effects are necessarily less important than primary ones in the economic field. To take a somewhat different example, it is evident that the full consequences of agricultural derating may take a long time to reach the landowner or the distributor of agricultural produce, or to wreak its full effects upon industry generally, through the redistribution of burdens upon the whole body of ratepayers who do not enjoy the farmer's exemption; but its repercussions in these quarters may be quite as important as its direct effect upon the farmers themselves.

Now the longer the period that must elapse between cause and effect, the larger looms the possibility that some new disturbing factor will escape from the compound of *ceteris paribus* before the effects of any given cause have been fully realized. And even the most superficial inspection of actual economic life at once brings to light such a welter of potential disturbances as to make the outlook for useful analysis look rather dim. For here we have to remember that what the analytical market economist takes as his data does in reality comprise an enormous number of highly changeable factors. All the myriad changes in the relative scales of preferences which initiate market movements on the side of demand lie in wait to disturb his original premises. Equally is he at the mercy of changes in the technical conditions of supply. And in the restless economic world that we know, changes in these spheres occur almost incessantly. Fashions in consumption come and go, cornflakes drive out herrings, herrings drive out eggs, and so on and so on. New machines and new processes disturb the relative costs of production every day; and again and again the refusal of *cetera* to remain *para* deflects the course of events from any recognizable relation to that charted by the clean logic of pure theory.

In the light of all this it is hardly surprising that the economic system proves very intractable to satisfactory analysis by the economist's conventional methods. If every market movement sets up a chain of consequences of indefinite duration (indeed it might well be argued that there is literally no end to the readjustments provoked by any single change, such as an increase in the relative preference for this or that commodity); and if, further, hard on the heels of one movement another promptly follows—then it is not to be wondered at if the economist finds himself in the position of "having to run as fast as he can in order to stay in the same place." Adapting an analogy used by Marshall in another connection, we may liken the economist to a man who is trying to explain the position of a number of balls that are piled in a basin in such a way that the lie of any one is collectively determined by the position of all; but who is struggling to do this while someone is picking up one ball after another so rapidly that there is no time for the others to come to a position of rest between one disturbance and the next. Or, to change the image, one is reminded of a baby chasing a ball which a mischievous adult continually intercepts and throws in some new direction. The unfortunate infant may indeed set off on what, *at the time*, is an appropriate course; but that course always becomes irrelevant before the object in view has been achieved. In consequence, his efforts are doomed to perpetual frustration, and unless he can find some way either of outpacing his companion or of anticipating the next move, he has no more chance of catching the ball, than if he never bestirred himself at all.

The possibility that our economic mechanism is so kinetic, that the rate at which new disturbance occurs is habitually greater than the rate of adjustment to such disturbances, has also implications which affect the arguments commonly adduced in support of the economic *rightness* of the system, in the sense of its ability to provide that our scarce means are so used as to give us the maximum possible satisfaction.[1]

[1] See in particular E. F. M. Durbin's thought-provoking article in the *Economic Journal*, vol. xlv, No. 180.

Here, however, I am only concerned to point out that the changeability of the economic system affects its amenability to useful theory, quite apart from any reference that this quality may also have to its claims upon our approbation. For it is just this combined complexity and changeability in the material to be handled that goes far to explain that awkward gap between the tool-makers and the tool-users, which makes the latter so ineffective.

A further difficulty, moreover, awaits the economist in the fact that economic situations appear to have a peculiar quality of uniqueness. In a sense, of course, every situation whether regarded from an economic or a non-economic point of view is unique; but differences may be less, or more, important than similarities. One case of pneumonia, I suspect, has much more likeness to another than has one case of inflation to another case of inflation; especially if the inflations compared happen to occur in, say, China and the Argentine respectively. In practice the kind of thing that it is useful to know about in economic life is usually just the kind of thing which depends upon a unique combination of highly complex factors; and this is true whether we are studying the price of matches, or the prospects of employment in South Wales, or the effects of saving during a trade depression. It is the business of a theory to draft general rules that will cover particular cases; but this is only possible when the cases are not, so to speak, too particular. Extreme particularity is the economist's nightmare even when he is attempting to apply his analysis to a relatively narrow issue, such as the price of a single commodity.

The result of these difficulties seems to be that while economic theory has succeeded in producing a few very broad generalizations about market conditions which are generally accepted even by the critical public, the attempt to refine and elaborate these has been relatively barren of practical fruitfulness. That things are cheap when they are plentiful, that the prices of articles jointly demanded tend to move sympathetically with one another, that the price of either of two articles jointly supplied tends to move inversely with the demand for the other such article, that higher returns to any factor of production tend to call out increased supplies of that factor (subject in this case to even more than the usual number of exceptions and modifications)—these are some of the typical propositions in which basic market processes are analysed. Carefully stated, they are not often disputed either by economists or by others, and they are not unhelpful. But they do not take us very far.

And, even at its best, this type of analysis is open to the very grave objection that it is totally useless for the solution of quantitative problems. No doubt it would be a great step forward to know with reasonable certainty what *kind* of results may be anticipated from a given cause in a given economic situation. But even with this knowledge we are not much profited if we have no measure of the probable magnitude of those results. No doubt it is a great achievement to be able to recognize a concrete case of increasing returns when one meets it in the industrial world; as it is also a great achievement to be able to diagnose the circumstances in which asking for higher wages is equivalent to asking for one's fellow-workers to be deprived of their jobs. But how much practical value has this information unless it also gives some idea of the *rate* of increase of these increasing returns, or the *number* of people likely to lose their jobs according as a given Trade Union extracts an increase of wages of x or y per cent? All practical economic issues are quantitative, and a purely qualitative analysis will never be more than the crudest of instruments for dealing with them.

Obviously, however, the awkward uniqueness of economic situations, which makes their interpretation in terms of any system of general principles so difficult, is still more conspicuous when it comes to quantitative precision. Safeguarded with sufficient "ifs" and "buts," the statement that an increase in the volume of means of payment will cause a rise in domestic prices and in the value of foreign currencies may be taken into practical use; but the further proposition, so grievously needed by those who have to wrestle with the actual problems of currency management, that an x per cent increase in currency will cause a y per cent rise in domestic prices and a z per cent rise in the value of foreign exchange, cannot, in the nature of the case, ever be condensed into a general formula; while the difficulties in the way of producing a useful quantitative estimate of the influence of any specific economic factors, operating in a specific situation, quickly enough for this to be applied in practice, are indeed still more alarming. In the end one is left with a feeling that there is something a little odd about the study of essentially quantitative matters by essentially non-quantitative methods.

VII

So far we have ignored the problems which arise when we pass from the study of competitive markets to those in which there is an element of monopoly. The definition of the difference between a competitive and a monopolized market, in the sense in which this is important here, is that in a competitive market every operator regards the price of whatever product the market deals with as objectively determined by the cumulative action of all the other operators concerned; whereas monopoly appears as soon as any one unit, or group of units acting in conjunction, is in a position to make significant changes in price by modifying its own contribution to supply (or to demand, as the case may be).

Alone and unaided the local cobbler cannot hope to force up the price of re-soling shoes by refusing to do the job at the figure now customary, since he knows that, if he attempts to charge more, I shall just go round the corner to one of his more amenable competitors. All the cobblers of the neighbourhood, however, acting together, can dictate the terms on which they will consent to supply their services; although, of course, they cannot dictate the quantity of those services which the public will buy at any given price. If we think them exorbitant we shall simply wear our shoes longer, that is all. In the economist's language the demand schedule for cobbling still remains a matter objectively determined and outside even the united cobblers' control; as also do such things as the actual cost of labour and materials required for the various jobs that cobblers do. But the establishment of monopoly amongst cobblers has brought one important factor in the market out of the objective into the subjective sphere; from now on the price of cobbling is whatever the cobblers think will pay them best.

Now it is a commonplace that the competitive market of the textbooks never becomes incarnate in all its stainless purity. It was never regarded as more than an approximation, or a potentially illuminating abstraction; and it is equally a commonplace that its purity has, in practice, shown a tendency to become increasingly sullied. And there are good enough reasons why this should happen; for it does not take any very profound insight to discern the advantages of successful monopoly. There may indeed be many practical difficulties in the way of monopolizing particular markets, such as the jealousy and distrustfulness of the various competitors; the absence of any one unit with the enterprise or the means to absorb or destroy all the others; or the hostility of public opinion. But since a monopolist is always in a more advantageous position than a competitor among competitors, we are justified in saying that there is always a certain instability about the state of competition, and an inherent tendency for competitive markets to become monopolized. It has indeed been well argued that the assumption that competitors have sufficient foresight to adapt their behaviour intelligently, on the lines postulated by equilibrium theory, to the vagaries of market movements, and yet not enough foresight to see how by combination they might themselves dominate those movements to their own advantage—that this assumption has too much nicety to be convincing.[1]

It follows that, as has already been said, the ten-

[1] Durbin, *Economic Journal*, vol. xlv, No. 180.

dency of the modern economist to take imperfect competition, or partial monopoly, rather than pure competition as the norm, certainly brings the theorist closer to the world as we know it. This practice might, therefore, be regarded as a step towards closing the gap between the tool-makers and the tool-users; and I for one should not deny that, so long as we stick to the traditional methods of economic analysis, it was a very proper step to take. But at the same time we have to realize that there is a sense in which every encroachment of monopoly upon a competitive system narrows the field in which the economist's tools can ever be applied at all. For the study of problems of monopoly or restricted competition must mean in effect *either* the study of the behaviour of the monopolist within a predominantly competitive world; *or* the study of the effect of certain islands of monopoly upon a system otherwise competitive. The first line of enquiry may be illustrated by recalling the case of the cobblers instanced above. Now, *given* that the cobbler's costs are objectively determined in markets where neither cobbler (nor anybody else for that matter) is king, it is possible to produce a set of principles explaining what sort of behaviour is to be expected from the united cobblers on the assumption that they are trying to get the best out of their scarce means. They will, of course, try so to fix the price of their services that price charged multiplied by quantity sold will give a maximum surplus over aggregate costs. In the light of this objective they will weigh the advantages of limited sales at high prices against those of larger output and lower price. But the important point is that generalization is only possible because the cobblers are still masters only of a very narrow field, and because, outside that field, the rule that the market is ruler of man and not man ruler of the market still holds. All the cobblers' calculations, in particular, are made upon the assumption that their customers are wholly innocent of any attempt at combined action; and that nobody, who is personally prepared to pay 5s. for having his shoes soled, will refuse to do so because he can rely upon everybody else doing the same, and so hopes to force the cobblers to do the job for 4s. 6d.

As, however, competition becomes increasingly restricted, the possibility of cases arising in which monopoly meets monopoly has increasingly to be reckoned with. The final consumer of such a product as boot-repairing would clearly be most difficult to organize, and, therefore, in such a market as this it would be ridiculous not to assume substantial freedom of competition among consumers. But all buying is not buying of final products, and there is plenty of room in the markets for intermediate products for serious restriction of competition among buyers as well as sellers. But wherever this happens, the economist's apparatus, however elaborate, necessarily breaks down. It was, I think, the late Professor Edgworth who summed the whole business up by remarking that where complete monopoly on the side of supply faces complete monopoly on the side of demand, "the solution is indeterminate." If a heavily-loaded pleasure boat sails up a narrow stretch of water where there are sights of interest on both port and starboard shores, you can state with confidence that at any given moment the boat will tend to list towards whichever side then offers the greater attraction; and if you have some reliable way of measuring the attractiveness of the various prospects you can even say definitely to which side the ship will list at any given point in the journey. But if the passengers are divided into two parties, each under a guide whose instructions they religiously obey, and if the object of each guide is to get his party on the opposite side of the boat to that occupied by the other, then "the solution is indeterminate." The analogy, for all its imperfections, may serve to illustrate the difference between movements that are a kind of by-product of independently-acting wills, and those that are produced by deliberate strategy.

The behaviour of the monopolist, therefore, is only amenable to rule so long as he operates in a non-monopolistic framework. And if it is also true, as has been suggested, that competition has an inherent tendency to destroy itself, this means that the field in which traditional methods of analysis can be fruitfully employed is likely to undergo a progressive contraction. Nor will this contraction cramp only those economists who attempt to apply their analysis to the behaviour of actual monopolists. An exactly similar limitation awaits those who elect to pursue the alternative line proposed, viz: the study of the effects of monopoly upon the areas not yet monopolized. Even granted that where monopolist meets monopolist the solution is indeterminate, we can still fall back on analysis of cases where monopolist meets competitor and where, accordingly, determinate solutions are still, at least theoretically, possible. The behaviour of the monopolists may, in fact, be taken as one of the many independent variables of the economic structure, like the public's relative scale of valuation of herrings or of any other commodity; and we can then go on to theorize about what will happen in markets that are nobody's private domain *if* our monopolists should take it upon themselves to do this that or the other thing.[1] But at the same time the potential value of such analysis *within the sphere in which it can be conducted* has nothing to do with the dimensions of that sphere. Such considerations cannot affect the fact that, in so

[1] Much of Mr. J. W. F. Rowe's valuable study *Markets and Men* is an admirable example, conspicuous for its practical utility, of the possibilities of work along these lines.

far as every encroachment of monopoly upon the economic system marks out fresh territory in which conscious manipulation replaces an impersonal mechanism, in which prices, supplies and consumption no longer "go" up or down, but are deliberately fixed at certain figures, such encroachment necessarily restricts the scope of studies which are concerned only with analysing the behaviour of that impersonal mechanism. Hence the economist who, with his eye upon the march of events, recognizes the appearance of monopoly, and virtuously sets out to devise a technique for dealing with this, must by that very act confess that the validity of his basic postulate is becoming more and more closely circumscribed.

VIII

All that has been written above about monopoly applies with even greater force to all those disturbances of market process which are set up by the deliberate intervention of some organ of State—with *greater* force because, whereas those who, as monopolists, attempt to restrict competition may reasonably be presumed to do so with the characteristic economic intention of making their own scarce means go further in that way, no such simplicity of motive can be ascribed to public bodies. The motives, ranging from self-sufficiency to protection of the poor, from "taking the profit out of war" to subsidizing the private manufacture of arms, are as varied as the actual forms of legislative interference. Hence, whereas in the case of our united cobblers it could reasonably be predicted that the union would use its mastery of the market to promote the economic advantage of its members, there is no saying with what intention some Government may not legislate itself into control of a market, nor how it may not use that control once acquired. And it is a commonplace that every day the inroads of State regulation upon our economic mechanism become more and more extensive and complex; until even in communities which still profess to rely upon the incentive of profit to keep their economic mechanism in gear, the question: when is a market not a market? begins to sound quite pertinent. One has only to refer to such controls as the restriction of output under our Coal Mines Act, to the Potato Board's power of excluding from the market potatoes which slip through a sieve of a given mesh, or to our whole mass of Labour Legislation, to be well-flooded with examples from this country alone. And in such states as Germany one may well ask what is to become of the economist's laws of supply and demand when the farmer is compelled by law to produce a certain quantity of grain, whether he wants to or not; and when the price of this, and indeed of nearly everything that he may wish to sell or buy is fixed, not by the interaction of market forces, but by the fiat of some official; or when the death penalty is threatened against those who attempt to follow the economist's principles in the foreign exchange markets? The old saying that you cannot alter the laws of economics by legislation is only a partial truth. Nothing is easier, or more frequently accomplished, than the prevention or the modification, by law, of the reactions that the economic system might be expected to show to a given stimulus in the absence of such legislation. Thus, we depart from the gold standard, and, in accordance with economic theory, substantial sales of sterling are anticipated. But the sales may be prevented by the imposition of an official (or even an unofficial or "gentleman's") ban upon the purchase of foreign exchange in this country. So long, indeed, as any corner, or any process, in the economic world remains immune from authoritative regulation, it will still be true that the consequences of regulation will be reflected in market movements outside the area which is itself forcibly subject to such regulation. In that sense it is true that you cannot legislate economic consequences out of existence. What you *can* do by legislation is to substitute one set of consequences for another, to prevent, or to divert, "normal" reactions; as when the imposition of a legal minimum wage leads to increased employment of juvenile labour not entitled to the full wage, or to the dismissal of the elderly and the not-so-bright, who are not thought by their employers to be worth the minimum required by law.

Hence just as the impact of monopoly upon non-monopolized factors in the market offers a field for investigation by traditional economic methods, so also can the economist exercise his subtlety in tracing the market consequences of legal manipulation of economic affairs. At the same time, however, it has always to be borne in mind, that, the more vigorous and extensive the interference of public bodies in economic life becomes (and their ardour nowhere shows much sign of cooling), the larger also becomes the field about which the economist can never hope to make any generalizations whatever—the field, that is, in which it is the will of the dictator or of Parliament or of the civil servant which determines events, in place of the inexorable impersonal mechanism of the market. And of all the miscellany which has to be impounded in *ceteris paribus* during the progress of the economist's analysis, there is no factor more unruly, and more liable to escape, than that of governmental control over economic life. So while the economist is busy reforming his tools for the study of the equilibrating or disequilibrating forces of the market, the Government and the monopolist between them are fast working themselves into a position in which the market will do what they tell it to do, and in which that will be all that there is to be said.[1] And the upshot of it all looks like being an economic theory which at best will be in a position to tell us what consequences may be expected to follow what effects if something (which will in fact happen) does not happen to obviate these effects; and if, further, the presumed consequences are not prevented (as in fact they will be prevented) from occurring by law. Which, perhaps, is after all not so very inaccurate a picture of the actual state of economic theory to-day.

IX

We may now pass to examine a rather different set of problems which would appear to have something to do with the failure of the contemporary economist to provide a tool-box that proves serviceable to the practical man. These originate in the economist's primary assumptions about scarcity. Here we touch upon what are surely the most fundamental of all his fundamental postulates. Is not the economist only called an economist because he deals with things that have to be economized? And what conceivable purpose can there be in economizing anything unless on the ground that in some sense or other there is not enough of it to go round? The Robbinsian school, as we have seen,

[1] Which raises the still larger, but related, problem, of what is to become of the economist in the fully "planned" society?

would define economics as the study of the disposal of *scarce* means between alternative uses; while those who are brought up in the Marshallian-Pigouian tradition learned at a very early stage to discriminate between economic and non-economic goods, by the test that the former are scarce, while the latter, though perhaps in some philosophic sense no less good, are sufficiently abundant to satisfy every need for them.

This implication of scarcity necessarily underlies all the traditional analysis of value, or of market processes, and in its absence the notion of equilibrium, and therewith what is known as "equilibrium economics", ceases to have any meaning. The prospect of higher profit will attract more capital, says the economist, and the prospect of higher wages will attract more labour (*ceteris paribus!*) into the industry in which this prospect occurs. Why? Because capital or labour cannot be in two places at once, and naturally wishes to be in the place that is most remunerative. Thus comparative rates of earnings serve to equilibrate supply as between the various alternatives in which labour and capital can be used. Even where the prospect of a good return causes new capital (or—less probably—new labour) to come into existence, it is still true that the cost of creating this new capital means, in effect, the sacrifice of something else. In the case of new capital this sacrifice consists, presumably, in the diversion of reserves from the manufacture of consumption goods to the manufacture of capital goods, with a consequent immediate reduction in the output of consumption goods. (In the event of new labour being created in response to a higher rate of return, we must, I suppose, imagine that the immediate sacrifice involved is that of parents who must do without sundry luxuries, large or small, when an increase in the family is contemplated.)

Again, the theory of international trade tells us that, in the absence of subsidies, tariffs or other machinery for interfering with market processes, each country will tend to specialize on those lines of production in which it has the greatest comparative advantages and *omit those in which it is relatively inferior.* In Britain we produce engineering products and textiles, instead of wheat and tea, importing these latter from other countries which can supply them more cheaply than they can our particular specialities. And in like manner as individuals we decide to become doctors *instead* of dockers, invest in armament shares *instead* of in shipping, because in each case the first alternative appears to us to be the more attractive. The basic principle of all market behaviour is that you cannot eat your cake and have it; have your baby and your motor car, be a doctor and a docker, invest the same capital in armaments and in ships, use the same resources to produce the nation's textiles and its wheat. That looks like commonsense; and yet the odd thing about actual economic life is that miracles apparently can happen—

that the basic assumption of scarcity does not always hold.

I am not, of course, here referring to those mitigations of scarcity which are made possible by technological improvement in this so-called age of plenty. Technological improvement has certainly increased both the actual and the potential output of industry in very striking fashion in modern times; but this does not affect scarcity in the economist's sense. In that sense a commodity remains scarce as long as the supply of it is not sufficient to satisfy all conceivable demands without any price whatever being charged for it—a condition which is hardly anywhere in sight of being realized, even if we imagine all monopolistic restraints upon production to be removed. Everything which has a price is by that very fact demonstrated to be in some degree scarce, even if its physical output is reckoned in astronomical figures. It is not the mere quantitative abundance of goods which imperils analysis based upon assumptions of scarcity. Nor is our traditional equilibrium economics disturbed by the fact that there may be "gluts" in the sense that supplies are left unsold in particular markets, owing to short-term maladjustments on the road from one equilibrium position to another, such as arise from the imperfections of competition, or the mistakes of entrepreneurs or deliberate public policy. These gluts are quite easily explicable in terms of the orthodox market mechanism for distributing scarce means, even though they may appear temporarily and superficially to belie the fact of "scarcity." Thus if my publishers charge too high a price for this book in relation to the public's grading of it in their scale of relative preferences, copies will be left in the warehouse; but this unhappy experience will play its part in bringing about a different *distribution* of such *scarce* resources as paper and binding-cloth, and the services of printers and other workers in the book trade. For Messrs. Allen & Unwin will set to work to divert the factors of production to supplying books of a type which they hope will command a better sale. There will be a shift from one *alternative* use to another.

The real contradiction presents itself, not when some particular demand has received a disproportionate amount of attention, but in the paradoxical case in which alternatives cease to be alternatives. If resources not used in satisfaction of alternative A do not in fact find employment in the satisfaction of alternative B, notwithstanding the occurrence of the appropriate movements in relative prices: if, in actual fact, resources are left quietly roosting or rotting in lasting idleness, then the whole Marshallian-Robbinsian analysis is put out of action. The existence of unused resources which have somehow got left out of the picture *but which may conceivably come back* into it, otherwise than in accordance with the orthodox responses to price movements, at once makes possible all the apparent absurdities of eating one's cake and having it, that were suggested above. The theory that a man cannot invest his capital *both* in armaments and in shipping, that the more that goes in the one, the less there is left for the other, is meaningless unless it is applied to the *whole* of his capital. Thus the habitual free-trader's argument that the adoption of a self-sufficiency policy in Britain, which increases our production of, say, wheat must inevitably diminish the scale of production of some article which enters into our export trade, say, coal, will hold only on the assumption that we have no wholly idle resources to devote to wheat growing, which would otherwise not be used for anything at all. If that assumption is abandoned, coal and wheat cease to be alternatives, the labour and capital employed in the new domestic food programme may not be withdrawn from anywhere else at all, and, just as much coal is produced as before. The only difference is that this coal is now sold directly to the new British wheat growers (instead of to the Argentine farmers whom they have replaced), or is exchanged for whatever foreign or domestic goods these British wheat growers may elect to buy with their new incomes; and the whole of the traditional theory of international trade, e.g. as elaborated at length by Professor Taussig[1] becomes ridiculous.

[1] *Theory of International Trade.*

Contemporary economists in this country do not appear to be quite of one mind on the subject of how far, or when, these topsy-turvy conditions really do occur in practice. Mr. Keynes's most recent unorthodoxy[1] has, however, certainly voiced a very widespread, if insufficiently vocal, uneasiness as to whether the scarcity assumptions of our equilibrium economics are not at some points decidedly fanciful. Mr. Keynes, if I understand his argument rightly, has postulated that in certain conditions we may have resources (in particular labour) unemployed, for reasons other than the fact that too much is asked for their use, and that this, in his phraseology, "involuntary" unemployment is something quite different from the "frictional" unemployment caused by incomplete adjustments to changing market conditions. The one represents scarce means on the road from one alternative to another, while the other undermines the whole assumption of scarcity. The argument is then developed to show (what must indeed follow) that if any part of these involuntarily unemployed resources can, by some magic, be got into employment, the resulting product will be a clear addition to the total national income, the spending of which will facilitate the re-employment of other resources also involuntarily idle; and far from it being true that the more you have of A, the less you have of B, it now appears that the more

[1] *General Theory of Employment, Interest and Money*, 1936.

you have of A, the more you will have of B and all the rest.

Now whether Mr. Keynes is right, or whether he is wrong in this particular issue, there is surely here material enough to explain a good deal of the inconsistencies and the ineffectiveness of contemporary economics. If he is right, then we have no reason to be surprised if theories that rest on a basic assumption of scarcity do not illuminate the phenomena of a world of which this assumption does not hold. If he is wrong (or rather regardless of whether he is right or wrong), then the appearance of such heresy in a high and very influential place will certainly split the ranks of orthodoxy, and lead to some striking contradictions in the opinions of accredited economists. (Mr. Keynes cannot, like Professor Scott, be quietly written off as "not an economist."[1]) One cannot expect people who set out from mutually contradictory assumptions to arrive at identical conclusions. If they did, there would be something very wrong with their logic.

It is perhaps worth pausing a moment to reflect how much, both of academic contradiction and of popular confusion upon economic matters, is to be traced back to this fundamental, but often unrecognized, uncertainty about the basic assumption of scarcity. The economists having for generations explicitly, or implicitly, defined the very essence of their

[1] See above, p. 24.

studies in terms of scarcity, have now been thrown into confusion by the suggestion that the alternative ends, between which they thought that we were bound carefully to distribute our limited means may, in certain circumstances, turn out to be not so much alternative as complementary, and that the very eating of our cake makes it easier for us to have it. No doubt they are gallantly setting about the job of trying to disentangle how far, if at all, these strange paradoxes do correspond to economic reality, and how far the old orthodoxy is still relevant. Mr. Keynes has himself suggested practical policies, chiefly concerned with monetary policy and the management of interest rates, by which he believes that the conditions of full employment of resources (i.e. of scarcity) postulated by our traditional economics might be made actual. His school are at least trying to define the respective spheres in which each of the two mutually contradictory assumptions now offered as the basis of economic analysis is valid. But until this job has been satisfactorily completed, it is not to be wondered at if the economists stand helpless before urgent practical problems. Until they know which assumption it is appropriate to apply, they cannot even answer such an elementary question as whether an increase in the total volume of employment is more likely to be brought about by increasing or by diminishing the general level of wages.

Meanwhile the lay public, without making either of

the two assumptions explicit, is in the happy position of being able to draw simultaneously upon both. Hence a whole set of theories based upon the complementariness of ends circulates cheerfully side by side with another set based upon the conception of ends as alternatives. The former comprises every variety of what may be called the make-work type of argument; while the latter are fundamentally orthodox scarcity-theories. Thus, at one moment we are told that the rearmament programme of our country is responsible for an improvement in employment. The production of A (standing for armaments) is in this case assumed to be *additional to* the production of E (standing for everything else), the latter being indeed actually stimulated by the expenditure of resources upon the production of A. The men who make the armaments are assumed to be subtracted from the unemployed, whom the community was previously obliged to support in idleness, and not from the butchers, bakers and candlestick-makers, so that no butchering, baking or candlestick-making is lost by this diversion to the manufacture of arms. But equally do we hear (and sometimes actually from the same sources) how the unfortunate German people, far from experiencing an armaments boom, are actually being starved by the policy of "guns instead of butter." In Germany, apparently, A and E are strictly alternative to one another. It is not denied that both views may be accurate, but it is plain enough that, if they are, there must be some vital difference, which cannot just be passed over in silence, between conditions in this country and in Germany.

Again, the advocates of spending for employment stand cheek by jowl (if they are not indeed often identical) with those who would wish to see the elimination of "uneconomic" middlemen in many industries, regardless of the fact that the uneliminated middleman enjoys an income which, after elimination, he will no longer be able to spend upon other people's employment. According to Assumption No. 1 (i.e. the scarcity-assumption) the resources now wasted upon the maintenance of unnecessary middlemen could *and would*, if distributive services were more rationally organized, be transferred to some more laudable use. The liquidated middleman would become a productive worker—e.g. a cabinet-maker—to the common advantage. On this assumption, however, those who "spend for employment" cannot be held to create any additional employment at all. The most that they can accomplish is a diversion of production into satisfying their particular needs in preference to those of somebody else. (This argument will be recognized as an old friend by those who are opposed to the inauguration of schemes of Government expenditure as a remedy for unemployment.) Assumption No. 1, therefore, hardly permits one *both* to frown upon the middleman *and* to uphold spending campaigns; for what more effective way of spending is there than the maintenance of an unproductive class? Assumption No. 2, on the other hand (that is the assumption of unused resources, or of no-scarcity) is a very proper rock upon which to build all the modern "pump-priming" type of policies. Let the Government get busy setting the unemployed to work on highways, on housing programmes, or even on rearmament; then, far from having to pay the price for these things in a diminished output of consumable goods, we shall actually be stimulating the production of the latter also. But this assumption, on the other hand, will not permit us to speak otherwise than tenderly of every unproductive person or activity. For from this point of view there is little difference between a useless middleman and a battleship. Both are conspicuous forms of supposedly prosperity-bringing waste.

Moreover the situation becomes still more complicated if we attempt to probe into the views of economists as to the mutual relations—in the real world—of the scarcity and no-scarcity assumptions. Mr. Keynes, as has already been indicated, appears to believe that by appropriate manipulations of the rate of interest we might eliminate all the (as they appear to the classically-trained economist) paradoxical absurdities associated with no-scarcity. Professor Hayek, on the other hand, has produced an elaborate analysis to show that the essential structure of our monetary system inevitably condemns us to a perpetual oscillation between the one condition and the other. In his *Prices and Production* he argues with the greatest subtlety that scarcity must inevitably resolve itself into no-scarcity: or, to express the matter more nearly in the terms which he would perhaps employ himself, a community whose labour and capital are at a given moment fully utilized is inevitably heading for a condition in which some of that labour and capital will become idle. The argument by which it is sought to establish this conclusion is highly abstract and intricate, and very difficult to confine in any summary that is both brief and lucid. In the barest outline, what it seems to amount to is something like this. Capital is ultimately created by saving, and hence, in the last resort, the distribution of the community's resources as between capital and consumable goods is determined by the extent to which individuals, or corporations of all kinds, do actually save instead of spending. This, however, is merely the *ultimate* governing condition that sits inexorably in the background. In the actual world its influence has to be transmitted through all the complexities of the credit system; for, as a rule, the *immediate* factor which decides whether or no any of us are going to create capital goods is our ability to command credit. Instead of undertaking the necessary saving ourselves we borrow a title to the resources which somebody else either has actually saved or *is supposed to have saved.*

Now this borrowing and lending business is where the banks and other credit institutions come into the picture. But instead of regulating the volume of their loans, and so of capital creation, by reference to the amount of saving actually available to support a given programme of capital construction, the bankers are guided by what, from this point of view, is an entirely irrelevant factor, viz. the liquidity of their cash position. That is to say, they keep on lending merrily as long as they are confident that they have enough cash in their tills to meet any consequent demands upon them. But cash in the bankers' tills has next to nothing to do with public saving. Hence the bankers' loans, which are the *immediate* cause of capital creation, are in no way effectively linked to the rate of saving, which is the final determinant of the community's preparedness to stint the present in the interests of the future, i.e. to pay the inevitable price of capital construction; and so there arises a persistent tendency for capital goods to be created, which are unsupported by the necessary saving—for which, in other words, there is no effective demand. In consequence these capital goods, and the labour which has been employed in their construction, are doomed to be wasted. When it becomes apparent that the demand for them is merely a fiction created by bank paper and completely unrelated to the current distribution of the public income as between saving and spending (i.e. as between demanding capital or consumable goods), this capital and labour must fall out of use and be left to rot in idleness. In other words the original postulate that all the community's resources were fully used ceases to be valid, and we find that what was labelled above Assumption No. 1 has now given place to Assumption No. 2.

This oscillation, it will be observed, from scarcity to no-scarcity, on Professor Hayek's interpretation, would not take place if the bankers did not regulate their loans in the way that they do. The fluctuation is due to a kind of concealed inflation (sometimes not even concealed). One must not, however, jump from this to the facile conclusion that the banking community are in a position, without more ado, to bring the actual economic world once more into conformity with traditional scarcity analysis. For their present mode of behaviour, with all its suggested consequences, is itself merely the result of their own attempts to distribute their own scarce means according to the most orthodox principles. The banker, with one eye on his profit and one on his cash reserve, is only following the ordinary laws of the market in his own particular sphere.

The layman, who may well find the argument of the foregoing paragraphs elusive, will perhaps get a clearer view of what this is intended to convey, if he studies the one pictorial analogy which Professor Hayek has himself permitted to relax the severity of the intellectual discipline imposed upon his readers. In our fruitless attempts to create capital equipment without facing the necessary abstinence or saving involved, Professor Hayek likens us to people living upon an isolated island who "having partially constructed an enormous machine which was to provide them with all necessities" subsequently "found out that they had exhausted all their savings and available free capital before the new machine could turn out its product"; and who, in consequence, had "no choice but to abandon temporarily the work on the new process and to devote all their labour to producing their daily food without any capital." Such, it would appear, is the eccentric and irrational behaviour which results in practice, not from eccentricity, but from strict orthodoxy on the part of bankers.

Fortunately, it is not necessary here to attempt a criticism of the merits of this hypothesis of alternating scarcity and no-scarcity, which Professor Hayek himself makes the basis of his whole theory of trade cycles, with their melancholy recurrence of periods of boom and slump. We are here concerned only with assessing the ability of the economists to analyse the actual economic world in a way that is realistic and productive of valid generalizations. In so doing, we arrived, in the first place, at the conclusion that our traditional classical analysis rests upon an assumption of scarcity of resources, or, in other words upon the assumption that, since we are already using all the resources that we have, any increase in the production of any one commodity or service can only take place at the expense of some other commodity or service. We now find that the work of two eminent, if not entirely harmonious, economists suggests that that condition is by no means always actually realized—a fact which some non-professional economists (to whom Mr. Keynes now makes generous acknowledgment[1]), as well, no doubt, as many a man in the street, have long more than half-suspected. And it cannot be too strongly emphasized that the non-fulfilment of this condition renders inoperative, irrelevant and unreal the *whole* corpus of economic studies as defined by Professor Robbins and as embodied in the classical analysis and its contemporary elaborations and refinements.

Even the very sketchy outline of rival theories given above will have made it apparent that the economists who have dragged into daylight this alarming rift in the foundations of our traditional modes of thought are not yet agreed about the reconstructions that must follow. At the present stage of the discussion, there-

[1] See *The General Theory of Employment, Interest and Money*, pp. 353 ff.

fore, the position which we have to face looks something like this: (1) Economics is the study of the distribution of scarce means between alternative uses. (2) In the real world this scarcity, with the consequent necessity to choose between competing alternatives, is sometimes real and sometimes imaginary. (3) Economists are not agreed as to why, or when, or how, scarcity passes into no-scarcity, nor can they offer any practical key towards determining either the limits within which the scarcity assumption is appropriate to any given concrete situation, or any general set of rules to be substituted for the traditional scarcity-analysis in the field in which this is inoperative. No doubt it is reasonable to hope that even these disagreements may be resolved in time, so that the disastrous consequences which result from applying a scarcity-analysis to a no-scarcity situation will no longer befall us. But in the meantime it must be admitted that to formulate an intelligible and practically useful set of rules for interpreting a structure which oscillates between obedience to two mutually contradictory principles is bound to prove an exceedingly awkward task.

X

The object of this chapter has been to account for a certain practical sterility in contemporary economic theory. The express apologies of some theoretical economists[1] and the habitually defensive attitude of many others are admissions that this sterility, though not necessarily permanent, is not wholly an imaginary grievance of the crowd outside the professional sanctuaries. Since the discussion has proved somewhat lengthy and intricate, it may be useful to append a short summary of the findings.

Our traditional economic theory, it was suggested, is concerned with analysis of the business of distributing scarce means between alternative uses as revealed in *markets*. The accusation that these markets are as much imaginary concepts as a world made of apple-pie did not prove to be well-founded. There are plenty of close approximations to the ideal market of the economist's textbooks to be found in the actual economic world. The really awkward difficulty appeared to lie rather in the essential nature of those markets. For practical purposes, relatively prompt solutions of actual problems are imperative. A glance at the intricate interrelationships of actual markets, however, revealed the following formidable obstacles in the way of prompt and complete analysis. (1) Practically every concrete economic problem is so complex as only to be covered by an almost infinite chain of hypotheses. (2) In practice, the effects of those economic causes which are farthest removed in logical connection (which often also implies geo-

[1] See above, p. 18.

graphical or temporal separation) from their originating causes are often just as important as those which are proximate, and it is, therefore, almost impossible to isolate any economic problem without gross sacrifice of realism. (3) The actual economic world is so kinetic that it may well often be true that the rate at which new changes occur is actually more rapid than the rate of adjustment to previous changes, so that the anticipated effects of given causes are, as it were, continually frustrated before they are even born. (4) Economic situations have an awkward quality of uniqueness which makes them most intractable to generalizations. (5) Practical economic problems are always quantitative, so that a method of analysis which at its best can only indicate the direction, but not the volume, of movements must leave off just where help is most urgently needed. (6) While analysis is necessarily dependent upon the movements analysed being objectively determined, and not subject to interference by the caprice of arbitrary wills, the encroachment of monopoly, on the one hand, and of Government interference on the other, is steadily restricting the scope of such objective markets in the contemporary world. (7) An influential group of economists has recently called in question the validity—or at least the universality—of the basic assumption of scarcity which is built into the very definition of classical economic theory, without, however, having arrived at an agreed opinion either as to the limits within which that assumption is actually valid, or as to how intelligent analysis is to proceed in its absence—with the result that we look like getting an economic theory based upon two mutually inconsistent assumptions, the respective scope of which we are unable to define.

Those who find these tentative conclusions at all well-founded will not, I think, be surprised that economic theory has not contributed more than it has to the solution of practical economic problems. There are, however, two possible readings of the situation as thus laid bare. The first is that the economists have not yet perfected their tools, and that we must wait patiently until they have, when all will be well. The second is that insufficient attention has been paid to the job which those tools are expected to perform, and to their appropriateness for this particular purpose. To me, at least, it seems that the second of these readings is at least as credible as the first.

CHAPTER 3

THE NATURE AND INSIGNIFICANCE OF ECONOMIC SCIENCE

I

THE somewhat melancholy picture of the achievements and possibilities of contemporary economic analysis painted in the preceding chapter raises the question how far economics is entitled to claim a place among the sciences. This is not, I think, merely a verbal matter. It is, of course, true that the important thing about any exercise of the human intelligence is what it achieves rather than what it is called. In the modern world, however, the title "science" carries a certain prestige—and for very good reasons. The claim of the economists, accordingly, that their work should be included among the sciences is in effect a claim that they should share in that prestige. Since the economists are already under suspicion of being charlatans, they cannot afford to arrogate honourable titles to themselves without proper justification.

I do not know exactly when, or by whom, the term "science" was first applied to economic studies. It is, of course, associated with those trends of thought, familiar to all, which have caused the period since the mid-nineteenth century to be described as the age of science. The use of the term "economic science," moreover, seems to be on the increase, and to be in a fair way to supersede the more modest "economics," much as this, in an earlier generation, in its turn ousted its predecessor "political economy." And it is, I think, hardly open to dispute that in the increasingly common application by theoretical economists of the term "science" to their studies there is an element of wish-fulfilment. For, while workers in the natural sciences may not always refer to one another in very flattering terms, they are, as a body, at least immune from the general public contempt which we have found to be, so often, the lot of the economist.

II

This is not the place to embark upon a full-dress philosophic discussion of the definition of science and scientific method. Definitions—at least of terms in general use—are concerned with the circumference of concepts, about the centre of which there is not likely to be any dispute. It is by reference to the essential, generally recognized, qualities of scientific work that the achievements and the methods of the economists must be judged. Now some of these qualities have to do primarily with method, others with results. In the field of method, the distinguishing characteristic of science would appear to be close and accurate observation of phenomena. Analytical economists, however, are distinguished, not so much by their interest in, and attention to, phenomena, as by their indifference to, if not their contempt for, many of the laborious observations undertaken by some of their more worldly colleagues. Some may indeed admit that realistic studies have their place as a means of tentative corroboration of "pure" theory, or even that inspection of the world of economic phenomena may suggest some of the hypotheses which it is the theoretician's business to elaborate.[1] But the suggestion that concrete observation is fruitful in anything like the same sense as analytical speculation is apt to be indignantly rebutted.[2]

If by this is meant merely that no intelligent enquirer in any field continues indefinitely to compile observations, without having some hypothesis in mind to guide his selection from the bewildering variety of phenomena open to his view—then it would be difficult to quarrel with the statement. The practice, however, as well as the theory of contemporary economists seems to suggest that this simple platitude by no means fully expresses their attitude on the subject of the part to be played by direct observation in their work. For in economic studies there appears to be, at best, a curious divorce between theory and observation.

[1] See Robbins, *Nature and Significance of Economic Science*, pp. 112 ff.

[2] Ibid.

On the one hand we have the meticulous authors of factual and statistical studies,[1] and on the other, carefully segregated, are the *a priori* deductive theorists. Now the latter habitually produce treatises in which *everything* is built upon hypothesis[2] and in which the only part played by the world of phenomena is that of suggesting the hypothesis, the hypothetical consequences of which are to be elucidated (and for this purpose no very close observation is required!). Thus market analysis is, as we have seen, based upon a broad general view of the principles governing human behaviour in actual market situations; and the theorist's pages are spattered with such hypotheses as . . . "suppose a substitute for the commodity in question to be invented," or "suppose a tax to be imposed upon it" in preference to "suppose all the world were made of apple-pie." But the curious division of labour, by which a group of theorists specializes only upon elaborating the potential effects of potential (if quite

[1] For such work at its most accomplished, see e.g. Clark, *National Income and National Outlay.*

[2] A good example is Professor Hayek's *Prices and Production* already referred to. The author, who refers caustically to the type of explanation of trade cycles which "depends upon a specious appeal to facts" (p. 30), sets out himself to explain these cycles on the assumption that "all available resources are fully employed." His justification for this procedure (p. 32) is that "if we are to proceed systematically . . . we must *start with a situation which is already sufficiently explained by the general body of economic theory.*" (Italics mine.)

likely or even historically actual) events, without feeling any responsibility for a continual reference back to actuality is, so far as I know, unparalleled in the methods of the sciences as ordinarily so-called. It results, indeed, in a very imposing array of technical instruments, in elaborate geometrical and mathematical presentations—some of which seem to bear about the same relationship to the natural scientist's curves and formulae as non-representational art bears to photography! But the zealous student of economic "science" would do well from time to time to remind himself that, of all the demand and supply schedules, cost curves or indifference curves that give so formidable an appearance to his textbooks, not one (unless by accident) is founded upon fact.

Nor is the significance of this difference between the characteristic method of the economist and that of the natural scientist destroyed by the unquestionable fact that the former is denied access to the most fruitful of all the modes of observation that are employed in the natural sciences. As an instrument for testing an hypothesis there is nothing to equal controlled experiment; and from this the economist is debarred by the very nature of his material. Condemned to such bastard forms of experimentation as "The Alberta Experiment in Social Credit," or the "Soviet Experiment" or even an "Experimental Tariff or Subsidy," it is small wonder if the economist sometimes looks with envy at the white-coated research workers in the laboratories of his colleagues; nor is it unreasonable that he should adduce his own lack of these vital tools as explanation of much that he may have left undone. To plead, however, that those who are precluded from using the typical methods of science should, none the less, hold their rank as scientific workers undiminished hardly seems good logic. One cannot have it both ways. Those who can use the methods of science to achieve the results of science are entitled to the name of science; but those who are denied (or scorn) the methods can hardly hope, either to achieve the results, or to be honoured with the name.

And as for results, it is, of course, just the economist's failure to produce what are generally regarded as the typical achievements of the scientific method that makes his designation as a man of science look a trifle ludicrous. Ultimately, public respect for scientific work is based upon the scientist's ability to produce reliable predictions on matters within the plain man's experience. As long as the aeroplane, the refrigerator, the telephone, the anaesthetic and the radio behave as we expect them to behave, we have little call to question the validity of the sciences by which these miracles have been made possible; and our confidence is still further confirmed by the fact that when the habitual predictions prove themselves false, when the refrigerator grows warm or the telephone dumb, or when the aeroplane will not rise—then application of the same set of scientific principles as went to the making of these things can usually be relied upon to set them right. We believe in this kind of science for the simple and satisfying reason that it works.

Admittedly, all predictions in the acknowledged sciences have not the same degree of reliability. The metereologist's prediction of a thunderstorm does not carry the same conviction as the astronomer's prediction of an eclipse. And there are sciences such as biology or geology in which the amount of successful prediction is as yet very small; which are occupied with classification of phenomena, or with hypothetical explanations of the past, rather than with forecasts of the future. Even these, however, are still distinguished by the characteristic methods of science, by their precise observation of phenomena and their continual checking of hypotheses by reference thereto. It is the plain man's knowledge that these methods have proved so efficacious in so many other studies of the universe in which we live, which keeps alive his expectation that here, too, the collection and analysis of sufficient data may in time, and on occasion, make prediction possible; and already the trickle of predictions, even from such sciences as biology, if insignificant beside that produced by physics or chemistry, is substantial enough to make that expectation look not altogether unreasonable.

The reader, however, would search far and wide through the works of the analytical economists before he came upon a single prediction endorsed by the weight of authoritative opinion of the course of events to be anticipated in any concrete historical situation—and with reason, for one cannot predict the future of a situation without looking at it; and accordingly, those branches of economic studies which deal with the hypothetical operation of abstract principles in hypothetical situations cannot, in the nature of the case, commit themselves to actual predictions about the future development of situations which they have never seen. The belief, however, that "important truths can be discovered by merely thinking, without the aid of observation," which apparently inspires the analytical economists (as it has at all times inspired the philosopher) seems to be far removed from the methods characteristically associated with science. As to the validity of this belief, those who observe the failure of the economists to establish important truths by "merely thinking" might do well to meditate upon the view that "this belief is true in pure mathematics because that study is essentially verbal"; but that "it is not true elsewhere because thought alone cannot establish any non-verbal fact."[1]

[1] Article by Bertrand Russell on "Philosophy's Ulterior Motives," *Atlantic Monthly*, February 1937.

III

Some of the difficulties, of course, which attend the effort to classify economics as a science are common to all those studies which are concerned with human behaviour. Laws are not laws unless they are obeyed; and the formulation of scientific laws or predictions obviously implies a certain orderliness in the material to which these relate, which will ensure those laws being obeyed, and those predictions being fulfilled. To the complete determinist who believes with Samuel Butler, that "the most daring flights of the imagination or the most subtle exercise of the reason is as much the thing that must arise, and the only thing that can by any possibility arise, at the moment of its arising, as the falling of a dead leaf when the wind shakes it from the tree,"[1] there is no problem here. Man, atoms or stars are all equally docile, and the kingdom of scientific law is made safe from challenge by the irregular or the arbitrary. Complete determinism is, however, a philosophic position seldom adopted by any except professional philosophers. It will hardly be questioned that the ordinary man takes it for granted that human behaviour is not determined in the same sense as is the course of events in the inanimate world, and that we do enjoy a freedom of the will which is not entirely illusory. It follows, of course, that those

[1] *Erewhon*, Travellers' Library edition, p. 257.

who accept this view implicitly set limits to the ability of any scientist completely to cover the whole range of human behaviour by any system of laws; that is to say, they concede that there are some matters about which prediction is, and always must be, impossible, not because of our ignorance of the appropriate laws, or of the situation in which they are to be applied, but because there are no laws to apply.

Since it does not seem likely that either direct observation or merely thinking will, in the near future, enable us to fix the boundaries of human freewill with an authority that is beyond challenge, it must remain a matter of opinion how far this factor destroys the title of all studies of human behaviour to rank as sciences. Common sense suggests that the choice is not between complete anarchy and universal order. There are wide ranges of human behaviour which show such consistency that laws relating to them may serve useful practical purposes. One may shelve the question whether behaviour in certain circumstances follows a given pattern because (in the deterministic sense) it *must* do so, or because wills which *could* be exercised in all sorts of different ways just happen all to be used in the same way.[1] For instance, the "law" that people

[1] Something of a similar issue arises, of course, even in spheres where determinism is generally accepted. Even in the physical world one cannot say whether it is chance or law or choice which makes things happen in the way they do. But this is the philosopher's

will tend to minimize the intellectual or practical or moral abilities and achievements of persons of whom they are sexually jealous, can be made the basis of predictions, the practical value of which compares favourably enough with, say, the predictions of metereologists about the behaviour of English weather. In the first instance, one need not question whether the tendency of sexual jealousy to pervert intellectual judgments is innate in human nature, or the result of social traditions that are made, and capable of being unmade, by man himself. One may believe in the freedom of the human will and at the same time believe that this freedom is often sluggishly exercised; and that that great variety of influences which may be vaguely classified as social tradition serves to inhibit a great many incalculable and unpredictable choices which might be, but are not, made. Most of us, indeed, would find it difficult to conduct life intelligently upon any other belief.

Ultimately, however, I do not see what useful purpose is served by obliterating the distinction between things that must follow a certain pattern and things that follow the pattern that people consciously choose that they should follow. One may, perhaps, distinguish three spheres, although the limits of each cannot be authoritatively determined. The first is the sphere

business, in which it would be both imprudent and irrelevant to meddle further.

of complete determinism, represented in the common experience, by the physical, chemical and mechanical laws, knowledge of which has given us the external apparatus of our "scientific civilization." The second is the sphere of potential, but dormant, freewill, represented perhaps by the consistent and predictable responses of particular groups of individuals to (among others) social, sexual or political situations (e.g. the tendency—in contemporary England—for persons of small means to address persons of substantial means as "sir," or the tendency to conceal lapses from strict monogamy or to applaud references to democratic government). The third sphere is that of complete indeterminism, or active freewill, represented perhaps by the decision that I am, at the moment of writing, about to take, whether or no to go for a walk this afternoon.

About *all* these spheres laws capable of sustaining useful predictions can indeed be made. Predictions relating to the third category are, however, clearly only possible in the form of generalizations about numbers so large that individual peculiarities cancel out. While it is not possible to forecast whether any given freewilled individual will marry or commit suicide, seek a Ph.D. degree or a divorce within a given period, yet it is fairly easy to estimate with reasonable accuracy the number of persons in any given society who, in the absence of any significant social change, will make such decisions at any time. Such predictions may have great social importance, but, being based upon observation, they have little to do with the *a priori* propositions of the economists.

To the second sphere—that of potentially active, but dormant freewill—we may suspect that a great part of the laws and generalizations begotten by such studies as psychology, sociology and realistic (as distinct from theoretical) economics should properly be assigned. The psychologist, for example, basing his generalization (like a true scientist) upon observation of actual cases, formulates a law that certain patterns of behaviour are induced by certain types of situation; while the sociologist may trace connections between various modes of living and the degree of knowledge of the technical arts of production enjoyed by a given social group. Such predictions, however, as that a man who has been nagged by his wife at breakfast will snap at his secretary when he reaches his office, or that the discovery of the possibilities of steam-power will lead to the rise of a crowded urban proletariat, plainly rest upon a large number of implicit assumptions, one of the most important of which, in many cases, *may* be that the persons *about whose conduct these generalizations are made are not aware of their truth.* As soon as he sees it as a blind reaction to his wife's nagging, the business man's impatience with his secretary may appear unjust and undignified even in his own eyes, and a more rational attitude may take its place; while a community which realized and disliked the anticipated consequences of exploiting steam-power might well decide, by appropriate legislation or modifications of property-right, simply to will those consequences out of existence.

Formally, of course, it is possible, by bringing into the light all their implicit assumptions, to express these sociological[1] generalizations in a form in which they can claim a validity equal to that of the laws which reign in the first, or completely determined, sphere. Given certain social habits, moral standards and so on, the exploitation of steam-power will as certainly result in the creation of an urban proletariat as water will change to steam at a given temperature. This formal similarity does, however, obscure a difference between the work of the sociologist and that of the student of the physical sciences which, to me at any rate, seems to have the greatest practical importance. For those who accept the view here offered that the sphere of active freewill is surrounded by a penumbra, in which the will is potentially free, but actually inoperative, may reasonably aim to push out the boundaries of this active centre into this penumbra. I recall once hearing an eminent psychologist remark that the essential process of civilization was just a

[1] This adjective is used as a convenient shorthand description of all those studies which are concerned with human behaviour.

matter of the conquest of the unconscious by the conscious, and that man will only be fully civilized when the unconscious is finally and completely dissolved in the light of the conscious. The psychologist's business, it was implied, is to promote this domination of the purely mechanical unconscious by intelligent consciousness. I am not competent to judge how far this is good psychology in the more technical sense, but the image here employed does seem to have an illuminating relevance to all studies which are concerned with any aspect of human behaviour. For the laws which the sociological student may formulate as the result of his observations are only comparable to the laws of physics or chemistry *so long as his material is determined in the same way that the subject-matter of these sciences is determined*; that is to say, so long as the unpredictable element of human will is either absent or inoperative. The very discovery of these laws, however, may often be a most potent instrument in the hands of those who would like to see that will aroused in spheres in which it has hitherto been dormant. As has already been pointed out, it may well be discovery of the truth of such generalizations as that jealousy perverts the judgment, or that steam-power production degrades the proletariat, that makes them cease to be valid. In the mechanistic, or determinate, sphere our dislike of the effects of causes cannot modify the link between effect and cause however much we may wish that it could, and try to persuade ourselves to that effect. If we wish to avoid the effects, we can only try to eliminate the causes. But in any sphere which is open to the intrusions of the will, the link between cause and effect is itself vulnerable. Disliking the effects, we can, if we wish, simply sever them from the causes; and whether in any given instance we do actually decide thus to sever the link or no, the fact remains that the investigator who has called the attention of consciousness to the working of an unconscious or unwilled process has inevitably destroyed the necessary, or determinate, character of that process. There may, therefore, be a real sense in which some of the most valuable work of the sociologist consists in destroying the scientific character of his own generalizations by the mere process of formulating them.

Hence, in spite of all that the student of the humanities has to learn from the technique of the natural sciences, with their emphasis upon thorough and accurate observation, and in spite of the deserved admiration which the name of Science to-day commands, there is significance in the differences as well as in the similarities between the natural and the "social" sciences. Nor is this just an academic matter. In the world of actual affairs the attempt to assimilate the two to a single pattern has, I think, been responsible for a fatalistic tendency which is practically mischievous, and tends to paralyse intelligent action. In this connection it does not matter so much whether the so-called laws of economics or sociology are correctly formulated (on their own assumptions as to the absence of operative freewill) or not. It is not the content of any particular law, but its claim to the authority of science, which is apt to be dangerous. The classical economist, tracing the relentless beneficence of the invisible hand, and the Marxian sociologist seeking to demonstrate how the social forms of each generation are as inevitably determined by those of its predecessor, as is the biological inheritance of an individual by the chromosomes of his parents—each of these alike, by his very claim to scientific status, diminishes the practical possibilities of his own work. If these (or any others) are indeed the laws of economics or of social development, then there is nothing to be done but accommodate ourselves to them. One may shelter from a blizzard, to be sure; but this is a very different matter from being able to stop it. The unmistakable limits of human freedom set by our physical constitution and environment are severe enough in all conscience, without its being necessary to go out of our way to make them appear more stringent still. In time, perhaps, when we come to recover from our present intoxication with the very name of science, we shall come to a juster appreciation than is yet possible both of the proper use of scientific method in humanistic studies and of the scientific rank of work in this field. In the meanwhile there is nothing to be gained, and much to be lost, by the indifferent use of the term "science" to describe essentially and fundamentally different procedures.

IV

The doubts just expressed as to the propriety of bestowing the title of science upon the study of fields in which freewill is actually or potentially operative take us far beyond the restricted sphere of the analytical economist. The ranking, it has been suggested, of *any* sociological study as a science cannot be conceded without reservations. But the economist's title as a scientist may be still further impugned upon additional grounds. For the laws which he evolves are contingent not merely upon the acquiescence of human will, but also upon the existence of a particular set of social institutions, which are far from being coterminous with the whole of human history and experience. As we have already seen, while the problem of distributing scarce means between alternative uses is inescapable in any form of human society, the "interesting complications" of that problem, which alone provide material for the economist's studies, arise only in those societies in which the matter is handled, in the main, by the mechanism of the market. In other words, the "science" of economics is a science of human behaviour in an exchange economy based upon freedom of contract, and upon property-rights approximating to the type that is familiar in the Western Europe or North America of our own time This, however, is a very narrow limitation[1]; and if it is taken seriously, in the light of contemporary trends in economic practice, it would suggest that the science of economics is destined only to a very brief flowering. For, as we have seen, and as is indeed a matter of common experience, conscious authoritarian manipulation is, over wide areas, increasingly tampering with that objectivity of the market process which is so essential to analytical economic "science." Now whether or no we concede that there can be a science of history or of sociology as such, there does seem to be something rather absurd in the notion of a science of a passing historical phenomenon. A certain quality of universality is surely implied in the very nature of science; and while there may be subdivision of the various sciences for convenience of investigation (as in *agricultural* botany, or *psychological* medicine, or *astro*-physics) unity is preserved in so far as (1) certain principles are common to each science as a whole, and (2) lines of demarcation that are based upon man-made institutions are not treated as having any greater significance than that of de-

[1] And it is very doubtful whether in this context Nazi Germany should be included in "Western Europe."

limiting the various spheres within which the findings of any one science may most fruitfully be applied and developed. If the laws of "economic science" were applicable to, at the least, a large proportion of all the varied forms that human society has assumed, or may assume, in its efforts to make the most of its resources, then perhaps their scientific character might be more gladly conceded; but if the "science" is dumb except in relation to the conditions of the Western world in the seventeenth to twentieth centuries, then it does seem to be an odd sort of a science indeed.

V

The aim of good terminology is to clarify, not to obscure: to reveal, not to obliterate, significant differences. The economist's claim, therefore, that his work is a branch of science, rests upon evidence of essential similarity between this and the sciences as ordinarily so called. In this connection we have found (1) that, whereas the characteristic method of science is close observation of phenomena, the economist rejects this in favour of umbilical contemplation; (2) that, in common with all other studies of human behaviour, the generalizations of the economist must be subject to disturbance by the unpredictable element of human freewill, and that, in consequence, law and prediction in this field cannot hope to attain that triumphant reliability which is generally regarded as the crowning achievement of Science; (3) that, whereas Science is a matter of evolving general principles and applying these in particular instances, the very generalizations of economics are contingent upon a particular set of man-made institutions (with a short history behind them and at best an uncertain future before them), so that in the absence of these institutions economic science becomes irrelevant, if not completely dumb; and (4) that, even within the limits of these institutions, the complexity and uniqueness of economic situations has habitually frustrated the economist's efforts to give practical substance to the ghostly form of his abstract generalizations.

In these circumstances the principles of good terminology would seem to indicate that the use of the term "science" to describe current modes of economic analysis is, at the least, premature.

CHAPTER 4

ECONOMICS AS APOLOGETICS?

I

We now pass from what is often called the positive to the normative aspect of economics; that is to say, to examination of the work of the economists, not as exponents of what does or will happen, but as counsellors about what ought to be done. This latter rôle is not indeed willingly accepted by all the theorists of to-day, notably by those who are most anxious to claim a scientific status for their work. Explicitly or implicitly, however, it is almost impossible for any economist who accepts the definition of his field as "the study of human behaviour in the distribution of scarce means between alternative uses" to avoid all reference to an underlying norm. He may, indeed, successfully evade the responsibility of giving advice as to the best course to pursue in any given situation. He may (and frequently does) say that, while he is prepared to offer an analysis (within his own assumptions, of course) of the possible results to be anticipated from the imposition of a tariff upon the import of shirt-buttons, it is not his part to pronounce upon the wisdom of actually adopting such a tariff. But even this purity of attitude can hardly be extended to fundamentals. For economics, as defined, is a study of the business of economizing—of making a little go the longest possible way. Its characteristic forms of analysis are only possible at all because of an underlying assumption that people do, in general, seek economy and pursue it—not, of course, necessarily always in any narrow monetary sense, but in the sense of trying to get the best out of *all* their opportunities in relation to *all* the ends which they think important. The pursuit of economy may indeed be conducted in an unintelligent and blundering way, but it must never be abandoned altogether if the economist is to acquit himself of the charge that he is dealing with an apple-pie world. For if people do not persist in the attempt to get the most out of their limited means, then there can be no such thing as economical action, and the phenomena which the economist sets out to study would lack that essential unity which alone makes them both intelligible and (at least after a sufficient process of abstraction) conformable to the generalizations that make up his theory.

It is, however, but a small step, and one which in practice it is almost impossible to avoid taking, from the assumption that people *do* try to behave economically to the implication that they *ought* to do so: that such behaviour is, in fact, rational, or intelligent, and so commendable. I doubt if any economist could be found who (aside from a mood of philosophic perversity) would refuse consent to the proposition that economical behaviour is also commendable behaviour.

Many, even of the most austere purists, at some time or other make the admission implicitly—even if only by taking pains to show that economical behaviour, if correctly understood, is not to be confused with mean or selfish behaviour,[1] since one may wish to economize one's resources in order that they may be effectively used in the service of the most altruistic or morally laudable ends. The ethical results of economic behaviour in this sense depend, of course, upon the ethical quality of the ends in the interest of which we are economizing. Here the pure economist[2] is indeed at pains to make it plain that he does not presume to pronounce upon the ethical quality of ends, or indeed to judge these from any point of view. He just assumes that the purposes that people set before themselves are purposes of which those people approve. But within the limits of this assumption, he can hardly do otherwise *as an economist* than commend whatever distribution of resources fulfils those purposes in the highest measure. Economical action, defined as the effective shaping of means to ends, is, after all, hardly distinguishable from intelligent action; and it is

[1] Robbins, *Nature and Significance of Economic Science*, p. 25.

[2] For criticism of this attitude, see below, pp. 246 ff.

stretching credulity rather far to suggest that those who are occupied with analysing the results of man's efforts to make use of his intelligence are innocent of any implicit judgment as to the propriety or commendability of such efforts.

In the last resort, then, I do not think we can allow even the purest economists wholly to disown the normative qualities of their work. They are in effect committed to approval of the principle of economy; and, even if they steadfastly refuse to interpret their precept in any actual situation, they must be regarded as upholders of one commandment "Thou shalt act economically" (because otherwise thou art a fool). The only difference between those economists who shrink from the presumption that it is their business to give all the practical advice that they can in face of actual economic problems, and those who share the attitude of this essay, is that the former do not accept the responsibility of *interpreting* the advice, which they cannot help offering, in terms in which it is applicable to any practical situation. They are like the pastors who exhort their flocks to be holy, but omit to specify whether holiness does, or does not, involve abstention from divorce, from Sunday games or from consumption of alcoholic liquors.

It should perhaps be added that, however extensive or limited a view any particular economist may take of his normative functions, all would agree that failure to distinguish between normative and positive propositions is wholly unpardonable. An "ought" must be plainly labelled as such, and in no circumstances slipped in under cover of an "is" or a "might be." In individual instances economists may be guilty of offences against this first canon of intellectual honesty; but it can be confidently asserted that there is no one who would defend the practice, even should his own record prove not to be completely blameless in the matter.

II

We are now ready to take up the allegation, discussion of which is the primary business of this chapter, viz. that economics is just a cunning system of apologetics for the kind of economic order under which most of the economists themselves are living. I do not suppose that there can to-day be any economist whose academic seclusion is so carefully cloistered that the sound of this charge has not penetrated to him. However ignorant and ill-founded it may prove to be upon examination, there is no doubt of the wide support that this estimate of "economic science" enjoys to-day.

Now the assertion that the economists are champions of our present economic system implies (1) that they are substantially agreed upon some norm by reference to which the economic merits of different actions may be judged and (2) that this norm is actually operative in that system, encouraging behaviour which ranks high according to its precepts, and eliminating that which runs counter to them. They must both know what is (economically) good, and at the same time be convinced that, in the system which they are supposed to be defending, the (economically) better is on the whole likely to prevail over the (economically) worse.

That the concept of such a norm does, in fact, pervade all the work of the English-speaking classical economics will, I think, hardly be denied. That it should do so follows logically, as we have just seen, once the admission has been made that economics is a study of mankind's efforts to behave economically. For these efforts are purposive: they are directed towards a goal, and unless one can recognize and define that goal (even if only in the most general terms) one cannot understand, much less give judgment upon, what is going on. It is just the concept of equilibrium itself which supplies this goal, inasmuch as it both makes economic activity intelligible, and, by the same process, exposes it to normative judgments. Economic forces are seen as departures from, and tendencies towards, equilibrium. Once a state of equilibrium has been reached, further movement ceases, *because the ideal has been attained and there is nothing left to strive for.*[1] (The fact that in a dynamic community the positions of equilibrium are themselves continually changing does not, of course, affect the argument, though it makes the practical application of both positive and normative economics desperately complicated.) The state of equilibrium is thus identical with the optimum[2], or supremely economical, distribution of resources in relation to any given system of ends; and, in so far as economical action may be identified with intelligent action, this state of equilibrium becomes not merely the objective which people *do*, but also that which they *ought* to, set before themselves.

As soon as this first concession to an essentially normative view of economics is made, the next task is to pursue this vague and elusive norm of equilibrium, or optimum use of resources a little further

[1] Of course all this is applicable only to an economic theory which is based upon the scarcity assumption. Once this is removed, the concept of equilibrium ceases to have any meaning as a norm. Disequilibrium becomes preferable to equilibrium, just as waste becomes preferable to economy, and all our traditional economists, both positive and normative, are flung into confusion. Hence, no doubt, the dismay with which the orthodox regard the attacks now being made by some of their colleagues upon the scarcity assumption!

[2] The frequent use of the term "optimum" in the writings of the theoretical economists is itself corroborative evidence of the impossibility of excluding normative judgments from economic theory.

into the realm of the concrete. And here the first step is a very small one, and one which even the most timid economists, whose phobia of responsibility for practical affairs is most acute, need not fear to take. Equilibrium is defined as a condition in which the satisfaction (in terms of a given system of ends) derived from the last unit of resources devoted to the promotion of every one of those ends is equal. Without entering into any of the more subtle controversies of contemporary economics, we may label this the principle of equi-marginal returns; and may thus define the economist's norm as the condition in which equi-marginal returns is realized.

For the benefit of the layman, who may not find this phraseology very edifying, it need only be said that this definition is equivalent to the statement that the economist's norm is attained when our scarce means are distributed amongst our various alternative ends in such a way that there is nothing to be gained by making even the very slightest change in that distribution: when to devote a little more to this end, and a little less to that, would make the result worse, not better. In other words, the job is perfectly done when it cannot be done any better. Incidentally, the foregoing way of putting the matter may not only be helpful to the layman: it may also assist the economist to realize just how startling a contribution to knowledge he has made by formulating this famous principle of equi-marginal returns, which in one form or other plays so large a part in his discussions. And, it may also help him to see that as promised above, the step from admitting that equilibrium is the economic norm to defining equilibrium as a condition of equi-marginal returns is both short and innocent.

III

Now equi-marginal returns is one thing for an individual and another for a social group. The individual is in the last resort sole judge of the economic quality of his own behaviour, for he alone can finally evaluate the respective claims of all the competing ends over which he has to spread his scarce means. If I find myself wishing that I had spent less time in writing this book and more in idling in the sun, then I, and I alone, am in a position both to diagnose the *fact* of this faulty distribution of my own scarce time, and to estimate its *magnitude*—provided always that this judgment is related to my own personal ends alone, and takes no account of the social consequences of my actions (e.g. the benefit or damage which I may confer upon the public by publishing such a work); for I, and I alone, can judge just how the pleasures of idleness compare (to me) with the pleasures of self-expression, or the prospect of acquiring fame or money from my writings. Hence arises that dearth of "interesting complications" which we have already noted in the application of equilibrium analysis (that is to say, in the practical interpretations of "equi-marginal" returns) in the Crusoe economy. Crusoe distributed his time between fishing, hut-building and reflecting upon the consolations of religion according to his own lights; and if anybody had come along and told him that he was doing it all wrong, he would be entitled to retort that he alone was in a position to pronounce upon that.

The problems of real life, however, are problems of social groups and, therefore, in practice, the application of the economic norm means comparing ends which are differently estimated by different members of a group, and many of which may not even be regarded as proper ends at all by some of those members. It is a matter of weighing cigarettes for you against learned books for me, or house-building against school-building, or reductions in taxation against more liberal allowances for the unemployed; and the whole fate of the economist's norm, the decision whether it must remain a beautiful theoretical dream or can be made incarnate as a guide to action, depends upon whether reliable machinery can be devised for reducing the competing ends of a whole group to a common denominator, in terms of which they can be measured against one another.

In a sense this is a commonplace to all professional

economists. Nevertheless I do not think that they can too often recall to their own memory, or too boldly expose to the lay public, the fundamental postulate upon which alone their power to apply their own principles rests. Economics is concerned with the principle of economy. Since economical action would appear to be synonymous with intelligent action in its own field,[1] it is presumably the economist's business to indicate how we may best act economically. Economy, however, means a proper distribution of means between ends, and its practical applications are, therefore, entirely dependent upon the possibility of accurate measuring of the importance of ends against one another. Only *if and in so far as such measurement is possible*, can economy be distinguished from waste, and normative economics become a practical reality. But should such measurement fail, the economist can have no guidance whatever to offer even to those who most zealously desire to practise intelligent economy. He can prate grandiloquently about the principle of economy, but he cannot recognize this principle when he meets it in practice. And should the measuring-rod employed actually be defective, inaccurate or in some mysterious way elastic perhaps—then the advice which he offers will be definitely misleading, and worse than no advice at all. Certainly, where an instrument is of such vital importance, little apology is

[1] I.e. excluding the scope of intelligence in the choice of ends.

needed for subjecting it to repeated inspection and overhaul.

Now of all the theoretically conceivable ways of converting the alternative ends of a social group into comparable terms, the market mechanism is one. In the market the desires, needs, hopes, aspirations of millions are reduced to a common denominator in monetary terms. Through the ingenious invention of pricing the urgency of your demand for cigarettes is compared with that of my craving for books on economics. Those ends which can exercise a sufficiently strong pull upon the market receive attention: those which are rated lower by that mechanism remain unsatisfied. And so the market serves the double purpose of at once creating and applying that measuring-rod, without which even the appearance of economical action is impossible. The necessary comparison between such competing ends as the production of silk stockings, of railway engines, of garden furniture or of margarine, is thus effected by the device of using movements of prices in markets to indicate just how the claim of each of these, and of a million other ends, is at any time to be ranked in relation to the claims of all the others; and our scarce means of production are distributed in accordance with the resulting valuations.

Here—in the operation of this mechanism—we have all the "interesting complications" which keep the economist busy, and are indeed the justification for his very existence. The generalizations of positive economics represent his attempts to show how the principle of economy works itself out by means of the measuring-rod fashioned by this market mechanism. But when he comes to pronounce normative judgments, that is, to estimate how far the apparent economy of the market is anything more than apparent, then he must face the task of examining the validity of the measuring-rod itself. If this is passed as satisfactory, then the link between positive and normative economics is securely forged, and we are entitled to say without more ado that the equilibrium positions of the market represent a true optimum distribution of resources. If, on the other hand, the economist finds reason to doubt the accuracy of the market measure, *as it operates in practice*, then it is still open to him, and indeed (if he believes in the normative significance of his work) incumbent upon him, to specify the precise defects that he finds; and to indicate in what conditions, if any, they might be eliminated. But if he should neither find the existing yardstick satisfactory, nor be able to suggest any means of making it so, then he has no alternative but to admit that all the noble army of economists, while with their imposing structure of economic theory they may analyse the real world, can advise only in one that is imaginary. For practical purposes their counsel is no better than that of a housewife who would draw up the family budget on the assumption that there were fifteen pennies in every shilling and eighteen shillings in every pound.

The suggestion, therefore, that the economists are openly or tacitly committed to support of the market economy or "capitalist system" as we know it, is just a way of saying that their economic theory identifies market equilibrium with the ideal equilibrium of the economic norm: that they accept the method of measuring alternative ends which the market offers, and accordingly regard the resulting distribution of resources in actual markets as a rational distribution. This is the primary proposition, the truth or falsity of which has to be examined. And to this is sometimes appended a further assertion, to the effect that this identification of market equilibrium with optimum is in some way disingenuous—that it is either surreptitiously introduced by implication, so that the reader does not realize what a momentous step he has been induced to take, or at least that it is reached without adequate and unbiassed study of the appropriate evidence.

To the first question, whether the economists do in fact regard actual market equilibrium-points as reliable indicators of economical action for the social groups in which they operate—to this question it would certainly be difficult to make an uncompromisingly negative answer. In a few cases the identification of market trends with economical distribution of resources is both explicit and enthusiastic. The classic example is here provided by an economist, who though not himself English, belongs to a school which has greatly influenced his English-speaking contemporaries—Professor Ludwig von Mises. In his work on *Socialism* (which he describes as a "scientific enquiry not a political polemic"[1]) Dr. von Mises accepts the definition of "economic" which we have treated in this essay as inherent in the work of contemporary economists. "Economic activity," he writes, "is rational activity. . . . It consists firstly in valuation of ends, and then in the valuation of the means leading to these ends."[2] He poses also the problem which has been indicated here, namely, that of reducing the conflicting ends of a social group to a common denominator; and explains that it is money which serves as this denominator, and "money computations" which are used in order that the disposal of commodities may conform to the criterion of economy. The one limitation upon the usefulness of money for this purpose is that it is inapplicable to things which are not exchangeable, i.e. which cannot be handled by the market process. In this sense it is, for example, in Dr. von Mises's view, illicit to attempt

[1] von Mises, *Socialism*, English edition 1936, p. 22.
[2] Ibid., p. 124.

to calculate the loss due to emigration or war. "But within these limits," he concludes, "*and in practical life they are not overstepped—money calculation does all that we are entitled to ask of it. It provides a guide amid the bewildering throng of economic possibilities.*"[1] And, lest the reader should have doubts whether money computations are to be identified with actual market valuations, the impracticability of economic calculation in a socialist community, which is innocent of any market process, is expressly contrasted by the same author, to its disadvantage, with the rationality of capitalist methods of calculation. "Without calculation, economic activity is impossible. Since under Socialism calculation is impossible, under Socialism there can be no economic activity in our sense of the word. In small and insignificant things rational action might still persist. But, for the most part, *it would no longer be possible to speak of rational production.* In the absence of criteria of rationality, production could not be consciously economical."[2]

The criterion of economic rationality which the author uses throughout is, in fact, that of the capitalist, market economy. The reader who will take the trouble to form a more intimate acquaintance with Dr. von Mises's thesis than is possible from a few brief quotations will certainly be left with the impression

[1] von Mises, op. cit., p. 117. Italics mine.
[2] Ibid., p. 119. Italics mine.

that (as indeed is implied in the word "persist" in the passage just quoted) the economic norm is effectively realized, not in some abstract ideal market, but in the actual transactions of practical life. Indeed, in the opening pages of the same book he will find a eulogy of the market economy, and of the success with which it contrives to compound, and to evaluate on strictly democratic principles, the conflicting ends of all the members of a different social group, which is so eloquent that it deserves to be quoted here at length. "Capitalist Society," we read, "is the realization of what we should call economic democracy. . . . When we call a capitalist society a consumers' democracy, we mean that the power to dispose of the means of production, which belongs to the entrepreneurs and capitalists, can only be acquired by means of the consumers' ballot, held daily in the market-place. Every child who prefers one toy to another puts its voting paper in the ballot-box, which eventually decides who shall be elected captain of industry. True, there is no equality of vote in this democracy; some have plural votes. But the greater voting power which the disposal of a greater income implies can only be acquired and maintained by the test of election. That the consumption of the rich weighs more heavily in the balance than the consumption of the poor . . . is in itself an 'election result,' since in a capitalist society wealth can be acquired and maintained only by a response corresponding to the consumers' *requirements.* Thus the wealth of successful business men is always the result of a consumers' plebiscite, and, once acquired, this wealth can be retained only if it is employed in the way regarded by consumers as most *beneficial* to them."[1]

In this passage the reader will note particularly the words that I have italicized—"*beneficial*" and consumers' "*requirements*," and the implication which they carry that this ballot of the market-place does actually distribute resources in a way that is economically commendable.

Laudations of the economic merits of the market economy as uncompromising as those of Professor von Mises are certainly unusual. Others are, or at least set out to be, much more cautious. The late Professor Marshall, for example, devotes a few paragraphs of his famous *Principles* to explicit discussion of the "general doctrine that a position of (stable) equilibrium of demand and supply is a position also of *maximum satisfaction.*"[2] This doctrine he finds to be true only "in this limited sense, that the aggregate satisfaction of the two parties [buyer and seller] concerned increases until that position is reached; and that any production beyond the equilibrium amount could not be permanently maintained so long as

[1] *Socialism*, English edition 1936, p. 21. Italics mine.

[2] *Principles of Economics*, 6th edition, p. 470. Italics original.

buyers and sellers acted freely as individuals, each in his own interest." The more sweeping interpretation of the "doctrine of maximum satisfaction," viz. that market equilibrium is a position of maximum aggregate satisfaction "in the full sense of the term" he explicitly declares to be "not universally true." In particular, actual market equilibrium is likely to differ from the ideal equilibrium of the economic norm in two important respects. First, the index of "satisfaction" which the market records (Professor von Mises's "ballot-box of the market-place") is only certified as reliable, in so far as it may be assumed that "the satisfaction which is rated at a shilling by any one" of the different parties to a transaction "may be taken as equal to one that is rated at a shilling by any other"; and it is further indicated that this assumption will be violated should there be great differences of wealth between the parties. A shilling, in other words, means something less to a rich man than to a poor one; and the market which knows no difference between a Rothschild's shilling and that of his gardener goes astray for just this reason.[1]

[1] Similar warnings against regarding the equilibrium even of a theoretically perfect competitive market as an optimum is given by Mrs. Robinson in her *Economics of Imperfect Competition*, p. 318. This work, which is in the main devoted to a highly abstract analysis of the *positive* working of imperfectly competitive markets, treats also of the normative standing of monopoly as compared with competition. And in this context Mrs. Robinson shows herself

The second fault which Marshall has to find with market equilibrium, as an interpretation of the canons of true economy, is of a more technical character. It relates to commodities "obeying the law of increasing return," the production of which beyond equilibrium-point "may cause the supply price to fall much." In the case of such commodities, market forces may cause production to be restricted below the level of which the principle of economical use of resources would approve; and there is scope here, in Marshall's view, for government actually to promote economy by overruling the readings of the market, and deliberately subsidizing production. How much this qualification means in practice must, however, be left entirely to the reader's guesswork; for, in accordance with the habitual custom of theoretical economists, the peculiarities of commodities obeying the law of increasing return are discussed at length in the passage quoted without any indication being given, either as to how these commodities are to be identified in practice, or as to whether they represent more nearly

refreshingly sceptical as to the economical virtues of even the best of markets, partly for Marshall's reason that market recordings will be perverted by inequalities in the distribution of wealth; and partly on account of a more fundamental philosophical scepticism, summarized in the statement that "it is not really justifiable to talk about maximum satisfaction to a whole population" since "to a strictly logical mind any discussion of utility to more than one individual is repugnant."

1 per cent or 90 per cent of actual production. We are thus left with the difficult task of judging the economical merits of the market process in the light of the knowledge (*a*) that this process is unreliable in the case of a certain group of commodities and (*b*) tha nobody can say, confidently, just what those commodities are; or even, it would appear, name any one of them, if only for purposes of illustration.

Such are Marshall's avowed criticisms of the reliability, from the normative standpoint, of actual market processes. Even his reservations, however, would not be accepted by all his successors. Professor Robbins, in particular, has recently attacked the view that inequalities in the distribution of wealth vitiate the market mechanism. Recapitulating Marshall's arguments, he writes "it is said, the more real income one has, the less one values additional units of income. Therefore the marginal utility of a rich man's income is less than the marginal utility of a poor man's income. Therefore, if transfers are made, and these transfers do not appreciably affect production, total utility will be increased. Therefore such transfers are 'economically justified.'" This argument, however, is found "on closer inspection" to be "merely specious." It "begs the great metaphysical question of the scientific comparability of different individual experiences." . . . "*There is no means of testing the magnitude of A's satisfaction as compared with B's*" where A has an income of £1,000 and B one of double that figure.[1] It follows, of course, that on this view there is no justification for suggesting that the market's distribution of resources, over which B has double the pull enjoyed by A, gives less aggregate satisfaction than it would if this inequality were eliminated.

In general, however, the view that economists do not distinguish carefully enough between actual market equilibrium and the ideal equilibrium of pure theory rests less upon their explicit treatment of the subject, than upon implied assumptions that lie between the lines. It is not so much any specific statement that is responsible, as the general impression left by the work and attitude of the economists as a whole. Having made clear, perhaps at some point, that the market process is only a broken reed, they march gaily ahead as though it was a stalwart walking-stick; and thus they lay themselves open to the additional charge of disingenuousness.

In the nature of the case a general impression can hardly be established or refuted by isolated quotations; but one or two examples may help to show how easily the impression that market equilibrium and the point of maximum satisfaction are interchangeable terms creeps into the texts even of those who are far from explicitly accepting Professor von

[1] *Nature and Significance of Economic Science*, pp. 137, 139. Italics original.

Mises's cheerful endorsement of this view. Thus Marshall himself, a hundred or more pages *before* he arrives at the express denial of this identification to which we have just referred, produces an argument which runs as follows.[1] A boy picking blackberries for his own consumption continues this activity up to the point at which "equilibrium is reached," that is, the point at which "his eagerness to play and his disinclination for the work of picking counterbalance the desire for eating." The satisfaction derivable from fruit picking is then expressly stated to be at a *maximum*. In other words this homely illustration represents truly economical behaviour in the distribution of scarce time and effort on the part of an individual. The next step is to introduce a second individual, thus bringing us face to face with all the difficulties which, as we have already seen,[2] crop up as soon as the problem of economy becomes a social, not a purely personal, matter. Here the author points out that, if the method of distribution of resources is that of barter, then "there is seldom anything that can properly be called an equilibrium of supply and demand." On the contrary, "the simplest cases of a true equilibrium value are found in the markets of a more advanced state of civilization."

There then follows a lengthy illustration of how equilibrium is attained in these "markets of a more

[1] Op. cit., pp. 331–336.

[2] See p. 141.

advanced state of civilization," where monetary calculation is employed. The example chosen is "a corn-market in a country town," where the price of corn is fixed by the opposing pulls of buyers and sellers at the point at which demand and supply equate. The example is realistic, and the higgling of the market which it illustrates will be familiar to every reader, no matter how innocent he may be of the niceties of economic theory. But the notable thing is that up to this point nothing whatever is said to differentiate the equilibrium of the corn-market from that of the blackberry-picker; or to suggest that the former does not have all the normative significance of the latter. In the case of the blackberry-picker, the point of equilibrium, we have been expressly told, is also the point of maximum satisfaction. In the community of the corn-market, thanks to the market mechanism's reduction of the preference-scales of individuals to the common denominator of money, there is also an equilibrium point. And every reader who was not influenced by ideas extraneous to the argument of the text would certainly infer that the equilibrium of the corn-market was also a point of maximum satisfaction, a fulfilment of the economic norm in just the same sense as is the equilibrium of the solitary blackberry-picker.

Subsequently one warning, and one only, is issued, against whole-hearted acceptance of this inference. It is pointed out that in the corn-market argument there is a latent assumption, viz. that "the marginal utility of money would be the same," throughout the whole process of price determination in the market. The lay reader, however, need not worry about the meaning of this technicality, since he is immediately reassured by the statement that "this assumption is justifiable with regard to most of the market dealings with which we are practically concerned," and that "the exceptions are rare and unimportant in markets for commodities," the one important case in which the assumption is not valid being the market for labour.

So much for Marshall. Since his day the interest aroused by controversies about economic planning has opened new opportunities for economists to beg the case for the normative merits of the market mechanism, under the guise of scepticism about the merits of the planned economy. One of the most frequent criticisms made against the planned economy—in the sense of an economic system in which the distribution of scarce means between alternative uses is not guided by objective market movements of prices—is that it would be wasteful, since it would have no criterion by which to gauge the economical qualities of its plans. Having no means of calculating what enterprises would, and what would not, pay, the planners, it is said, would, even with the best intentions, be liable to embark upon all sorts of undertakings which would be gross violations of the economic norm. In the days before the planning experiments of the Soviet Union were initiated, this argument generally took the form of suggesting that the wastefulness of a socialist state would exhibit itself as sluggish indifference to new inventions of all kinds, which the market mechanism of the unplanned economy brings into use by the simple device of bankrupting those who do not keep up with the times. More recently, however, in view of the apparent irrelevance of this criticism to the operations of the first large-scale socialized economy to be actually established, the economic improprieties laid to the account of a planned society have generally been of exactly the opposite kind. Planners, it is suggested, are liable to become madly technique-conscious. They are unable to distinguish between technical and economic efficiency; and, in their megalomania, they may (as it is suggested that the Soviet Government has done) rush to instal everywhere the most elaborate and up-to-date technical appliances without realizing that these are far too costly to be really worthwhile. They will thus be making the same kind of mistake as a housewife who might introduce automatic washing machines, dish-washers and internal telephones, suitable for a large hotel, into a one-room flat. The appliances are technically excellent but they are not economical unless they can be continuously used. And all this will result from the lack of any means of interpreting the norms of economical behaviour in a language applicable to concrete situations.

Now installation of machinery is in harmony with the principle of economy so long as the increased product which the machines make possible outbalances the cost of making them and of providing for their replacement; including, of course, in the cost of manufacture, the necessary "abstinence" arising from the fact that resources devoted to the building of machines cannot also, simultaneously, be employed in the satisfaction of immediate needs. In the market this formula is easily and effectively reduced to intelligible terms, reading as follows: the installation of machinery is economical in so far as the market value of the product of the machine covers the market cost of its installation, including interest and depreciation at the market rate. But what if there is no market to provide the necessary basis for all these calculations? Those who destroy the market mechanism at the same time deprive themselves, it is said, of the touchstone by which alone they can distinguish economical from uneconomical behaviour, and "rational action" becomes impossible.[1]

[1] For a full discussion of the kind of argument here briefly summarized, the reader should study all the essays in *Collectivist Economic Planning* edited by Professor Hayek. He should note the implications of Professor von Mises's forecast, repeated in this volume, that in a socialist state "in trivial and secondary matters rational conduct might still be possible, but in general it would be

Now as a criticism of a non-market economy this is one thing: as an implicit defence of the validity of actual market mechanisms quite another. I do not think that any fair-minded person would deny that the kind of criticism of collectivist planning which runs all through the volume to which I have just referred (and which is characteristic of the contemporary economists' condemnations of planning) is a criticism of contrast—of contrast between what is proposed and what is. It is not argued that a planned economy would fail to provide a solution of any *existing* agnosticism as to the concrete interpretations of the economic norm. On the contrary, opposition to planning rests upon the belief that it is definitely retrogressive; that it frankly substitutes the irrational for the rational, darkness for light.

It is so important that the attitude of contemporary economists in this matter should not be misunder-

impossible to speak of rational production any more" (p. 105); and Professor Hayek's own strictures (p. 205) upon the Soviet plans.

In this connection it is perhaps worth pointing out that there seems to be a certain inconsistency in the position of those who, like Professor Hayek, quote the Soviet Union as an example of a society in which the criterion for distinguishing rational and economical from foolish and wasteful action has been abolished, and then proceed to upbraid the Soviet planners for their *uneconomically* large investments in capital production. In the absence of any criterion, how does Professor Hayek know that the scale of these investments is uneconomical?

stood that I must ask the reader to bear with one more set of examples—this time from Professor Robbins's recent book on *Economic Planning and International Order*. The central theme of this book is that planning,[1] in the form of such national or international interference with market movements as is popular to-day, is ordinarily vicious, in that it induces a less economical distribution of resources than would result in its absence. Thus, speaking of planned control of imports (as by tariffs, quotas or export subsidies), Professor Robbins finds that the greater the elaboration of these experiments, the more "the division of labour is likely to be . . . distorted." "*There will be still more of the wrong industries in the wrong places.*"[2] Again, it is found to be a mistaken policy to attempt (as under some of the present schemes for international control of raw materials) to uphold prices in the interests of producers, for under competition "plant will only go out of operation if the cost of working it is greater than the prevailing price. *And if that is so, then it is rational that it should be abandoned.*" Finally, summarizing his argument on "partial international planning," Professor Robbins lays down that "the whole notion of making possible an

[1] In the sense in which the word is used in this essay. Professor Robbins himself employs this particular term somewhat differently, giving it a wider significance.

[2] Op. cit., p. 59.

orderly international co-operation by the equalization of wages and hours of labour falls to the ground" . . . because "relative costs are simply part of a market mechanism which shows how *best* the inhabitants of the different areas may earn their real incomes. . . ."[1] It is true that at one point[2] Professor Robbins does remark that "It is conceivable that a world authority with perfect knowledge might in certain cases have occasion to interfere with the free working of private enterprise." No examples are, however, given as to the possible nature of such occasions (no doubt because in the absence of perfect knowledge they cannot be foreseen); and we are left with the *presumption* that, in any given instance, interference with market mechanisms on the part of any lesser authority, or of one not endowed with perfect knowledge, must be pernicious, because, by shattering market equilibrium it distorts the distribution of resources from an optimal position. It must be borne in mind that in this particular book Professor Robbins is not mainly discussing abstract questions of theory. He is writing about what should be done, and in particular about the foolishness and wastefulness of much of what we are actually doing, and it is just our indifference to the canons of the market which is his measure of that folly and waste.

[1] Op. cit., pp. 139, 182; italics in each case mine.

[2] Op. cit., p. 55.

In such ways as these some of our leading economists do give countenance to the view that they are, at least in a considerable degree, committed to defence of existing institutions. And the public can hardly be blamed if it sees them in this light. For, supposing, for the sake of argument, that it could be shown to the satisfaction of the economist-critics of planning that market pricing as we know it is an entirely irrational and arbitrary business; that the price of beer, the rate of interest or the fees charged by physicians, along with every other price of any kind whatsoever, are to-day determined by a process no more rational than that of drawing numbers out of a hat, then, while they might not withdraw, these critics would certainly have to restate, their condemnation of the planned economy. To this extent, at least, they are committed to the implication that the market mechanism does represent at least some approach to an intelligent practical interpretation of the requirements of economical behaviour. The issue may perhaps be summed up in a simple analogy. If I am driving a motor-car along an unobstructed road with the intention of maintaining a given speed, I have the option of regulating my pace either by the readings of the speedometer, or by direct observation of the rate at which I appear to be passing objects by the roadside. If I choose the latter method, I lay myself open to the criticism that such observation (especially if it is not guided by a great deal of previous experience, itself based upon accurate speedometer readings) is likely to be very faulty and imperfect. But those who condemn my preference for direct observation as unintelligent, implicitly commit themselves to the view that the speedometer is connected with the mechanism of the car in such a way as to afford at least a fairly good guide to its speed. If they should discover that in fact there is no such connection, and that the movements of the speedometer-needle are simply governed by the jolting of the car upon the road, then they would certainly have to revise, or, at least, to restate their opinion. The criticisms of many contemporary economists upon the economic rationality of a planned society carry implications about the market mechanism exactly parallel to the implications about the accuracy of my speedometer that are contained in the judgment of those who, in the example quoted, would condemn my disregard of its readings.

In any case, whatever his particular views as to the actual relation of market equilibrium to economical distribution of resources, an economist cannot be too careful repeatedly to emphasize that these terms are in no way *necessarily* identical. The continual shifting of market demand, supply and price towards a point of equilibrium—that is to say, towards a point which, *given the whole pricing structure, is more satisfactory to both buyer and seller than any other point that they can discover*—is obviously *some kind of* replica of the process by which an individual seeks so to regulate his picking of blackberries, that he leaves off at the point at which some other occupation becomes more attractive than further blackberrying; and similarly also is it *some kind of* replica of the process by which Crusoe attempts satisfactorily to distribute his time and resources between the various competing claims, such as fishing, home-building, farming, upon those scarce means. Now the analytical economist, occupied with his "interesting complications," discusses the intricacies of this market process, with its endless quest for equilibrium (or "optimum") positions, in the greatest detail. If he mentions Crusoe or the blackberry-picker at all, it is just in order to show the formal unity of the principle of economy in all fields. Inevitably the reader, unless the differences are continually and clearly stressed, will find himself implicitly ascribing to the market "optimum" all the normative significance of the simple, personal optimum of Crusoe or of the blackberry-picker; and he will tend, in consequence, to slip into the belief that equilibration of demand, supply and price in the market produces maximum *social* satisfaction in the same sense as maximum *personal* satisfaction is produced by leaving off picking blackberries at the point at which you discover that you would rather do something else. It is the very neatness of the parallel which makes it so insidious. Hence the economist cannot, indeed, be too careful to stress its limitations.

When we come to the practical job of estimating how far market processes do actually give an economical distribution of resources, the significance of these cautions will only be fully appreciated if we have always in mind the intimate interrelation of the whole economic structure. For every individual in a market economy is surrounded by a network of prices which he takes for granted, and in the light of which, as data, he tries to distribute his scarce means economically. For example, I know that I must pay £1,500 for a particular type of house, £200 for a car, 3½d. for a pint of milk, a shilling for a dozen oranges, and so on and so on. *Given this structure of prices* I can (within limits) distribute my resources between the satisfaction of my various needs for houses, cars, milk and oranges with intelligent economy. But even supposing that my own behaviour is extremely intelligent and economical, its effectiveness in helping to produce a distribution of resources that is economical from the social point of view depends entirely upon the way in which this price structure is itself arrived at. If, for example, some of these prices are formed as the result of market operations which every economist would adjudge to be highly imperfect replicas of the Crusoe-blackberry-pattern; if, for example, the price of houses is kept up, and the supply restricted, by a builders' monopoly, then, this distortion will enter into, and bias, every subsequent market influence in which the cost of housing appears as a datum; and owing to the elaborate interconnections of markets, this single imperfection of the market process may mean distortion over a very wide field indeed. For high-cost houses mean high rents, and the level of rentals may affect wages, and wage movements will influence the distribution of production as between commodities in which labour forms a large element of cost (e.g. mining) and those in which labour cost is relatively insignificant (e.g. textiles). In this way any flaws in the market process are likely to be cumulative, and a distrust of market results, which in the beginning may have related only to a few isolated instances, may grow of itself into a complete scepticism as to the supposed kinship between the market process and socially economical behaviour. In short, even the most perfect arithmetic, applied to inaccurate data, is bound to give an inaccurate result; and if the sum should happen to be one of multiplication, any error in the original data will be actually magnified in the final result.

IV

So far we have considered only how far economic theory may fairly be described as a system of explicit or implicit apologetics, without more than passing reference to the merits of whatever apology it contains. The next step will be to consider on what, if any, grounds normative significance may legitimately be ascribed to the market process, either actually or potentially. And here we touch the most fundamental of all the questions that face the economist who seriously believes that his job as expositor is, in the last resort, secondary to his job as adviser. It is also a matter, incidentally, in which his own future is vitally involved (though let us hope that that will not in any way bias his reasoning). For, as we have seen,[1] market processes alone offer a field (even if not a very fertile one!) for positive economics—for the formulation, that is to say, of economic laws about what does or may happen in the distribution of scarce means between alternative uses. Now should this market process turn out to be a mere mirage, so far as the pursuit of true economy is concerned, as irrelevant to truly economical behaviour as are the speedometer readings of one car to the speed of another, then the economist who believes that it is his duty to promote economical behaviour has no alternative but to pronounce against this method of distributing resources by an objectively determined system of market prices. In other words he must disparage the only kind of economic system to which his particular forms of generaliza-

[1] See Chapter 2.

tion are applicable; and that, of course, means the end of him.

Effective criticism of the normative significance, actual or potential, of the market process demands another chapter. Before, however, we embark upon this task, it may be illuminating to set out here some of the more startling[1] results to which those are committed who accept both Professor Robbins's definition of the scope of economics, and Professor von Mises's whole-hearted endorsement of the normative significance of the market. Such are the following:

(1) *Those who engage in such activities as the burning of wheat or coffee, or who throw back a catch of fish into the sea, must not be said to be responsible for destruction of wealth.* For wealth, it will be remembered, is not a material substance like cheese or bread. It is an intangible attribute of commodities or activities, based upon their satisfaction-giving power, and is just as likely to inhere in immaterial things like religious exercises as in those which satisfy the grosser appetites. Now in a market economy, it will be remembered, the test of power to give satisfaction is supplied by the market. So long, therefore, as any commodity, say codfish, commands a market price sufficiently high to attract resources into the production of that commodity in preference to any other, so long does that commodity continue

[1] To the layman, that is.

to have the attributes of wealth. But when this (equilibrium) point is passed, further production of codfish is a violation of the principle of economical distribution of scarce means: far from adding to the total wealth (or realized satisfaction) that can be created by a given volume of resources, additional codfish actually detracts from this. Resources (men's time and the wear and tear of fishing-nets and boats) are wasted in catching these unmarketable fish, which thus represent not wealth, but negative wealth. The fish have been black-balled by Professor von Mises's "ballot of the market-place." Whoever, therefore, throws them back into the sea is completely innocent of destroying wealth. Indeed, we are even entitled to go further and, generalizing the principle here involved, to say that the destruction of commodities *cannot* be also destruction of wealth, so long as the destroyers are motivated merely by the normal incentives of the market, i.e. so long as it is done in the interests of profit. Wealth might be destroyed by earthquake or fire; but the destruction of wealth for economic motives is, strictly, impossible.

By the same logic, it follows that the supposed paradox of "poverty in plenty" of which we hear so much to-day, is also a figment of the imagination. For the plenty is only a plenty of not-wealth, not a plenty of wealth. To suppose the contrary is again to make the elementary mistake of confusing wealth with lumps of material stuff. Certainly, during the years 1929-33 lumps of stuff like tin and rubber and grain and coffee and cotton were being heaped up on the grand scale the world over; but the market mechanism did not register these accumulations as having the essential attribute of wealth, and this plenty, therefore, was merely a plenty of stuff and in no sense a plenty of wealth. There was, therefore, no paradox in this plenty co-existing with great and widespread poverty.

These conclusions should be very consoling to those who may have felt that their poverty was made even more unbearable by contrast with the abundance by which it was surrounded, or by the conviction that the wealth which they so grievously lacked was actually being deliberately destroyed!

(2) The next paradox reads as follows: *The provision of an income for persons who are unemployed diminishes the total satisfaction-giving power of our resources.* The aggregate satisfaction of the community as a whole would, in fact, if market norms are reliable, be greater if the unemployed were left without any income at all! For, again, it is the market which provides the sole test of the satisfaction-giving power of any given use of resources, as compared with any alternative. Now the social satisfaction derived from the expenditure of resources upon the remuneration of any *employed* person is measured by

the market rate of wages which he can command. A baker may get £3 a week, because the market estimates the satisfaction-giving qualities of the bread which he bakes, and of his particular part in the baking, at just that figure. But the market also estimates the contribution of an unemployed person to any satisfaction-giving line of production as precisely *nil*—so long as he remains unemployed. Nobody is willing to pay for his work, i.e. nobody can get any satisfaction out of his services. Maximum satisfaction, is, therefore, by this logic, diminished by the diversion to the maintenance of the unemployed of any resources which would otherwise have been used in the purchase of any commodity or service (however luxurious) that commands a price, and is, in consequence, officially labelled as satisfaction-giving. Now the money that I am compelled to pay in taxes for the maintenance of the unemployed I should have spent, were I not so compelled, on the purchase of, say, additional stockings or books. For these I would *voluntarily* have paid a price; and that price measures, for the purpose of guiding the distribution of resources in accordance with the principle of economy in a social group, the exact satisfaction-giving quality of every unit of resources devoted to the production of stockings or books. But there is no evidence that I would *voluntarily* have paid anything towards the maintenance of the unemployed; and indeed the fact that they are unemployed is evidence that neither I nor anybody else was willing to do so. To tax for the support of the unemployed is, therefore, according to market norms, deliberately to divert resources from a channel in which they are recorded as giving some satisfaction, to one in which by the same method of reckoning they are found to give none, flat in the face of the principle of intelligent or "rational" economy. The aggregate satisfaction of the community would thus be increased if we could throw the unemployed, like the surplus fish, into the sea! I am not, however, aware that this course has actually been recommended by any economist; but those who have observed the not infrequent cases of suicide recorded amongst unemployed persons will note that this is an opinion which the unemployed themselves too often share.

These results are so grotesque that if any economist has had patience to read so far he will almost certainly be on the point of throwing this essay away in contempt and disgust. If he thinks it worthwhile to formulate his objection to the logic by which these strange conclusions are reached more precisely, he will no doubt call attention to the fact that it is the glaring *imperfection* of actual markets which make both products and labour unsalable. In a market which had not been tampered with, the price of fish would adjust itself to the size of the catch so that not an ounce would remain unsold; and, as for unemployment, he might argue that, if the labour market were completely free, we should all get work, if we wanted it, though not necessarily at a rate of wages commensurate with our own private estimate of the value of our abilities. And for these imperfections in the market process, and so for the "surpluses" that result therefrom, he will ascribe the blame, not to the markets themselves, but to the stranglehold of monopolies, or the meddlesomeness of governments.

All this may be true enough. No man in his senses would wish to subscribe to conclusions as ridiculous as those set out above, nor would anyone in his senses wish to impute these opinions to intelligent and educated persons. But the point is, not that economists commit themselves to these opinions, but that they leave such inferences open to be legitimately drawn every time that they slip into the habit of using the market as a norm, without expressly making it clear that the markets which they have in mind are entirely distinct from anything known to practical experience. And the quotations already given show that, notwithstanding the increasing amount of attention paid, particularly by some of our younger economists,[1] to the positive analysis of imperfectly competitive markets, the tendency to identify market processes

[1] Again reference must be made to Robinson's *Economics of Imperfect Competition*, and Chamberlin's *Theory of Monopolistic Competition*.

with rational and economical behaviour is still deeply embedded in contemporary economic thinking.

With this disclaimer, we may append one or two more of the quaint results that follow from uncritical acceptance of market norms.

(3) *In a social group the decisions which are consciously and deliberately taken are the decisions which are most certain to be wrong*; and this holds irrespective of whether collective decisions are made through the agency of a dictator, or by some attempted democratic process. This is a pretty severe commentary upon man's ability to apply his intelligence to the problems of social living. Admittedly, the virulent destructiveness of organized political groups in the contemporary world gives only too much reason to suspect that there is some justification for such severity. But, whether justified or not, a criticism so harsh as this should not be left to lurk under an implication. If it is there, it should be brought out to daylight and publicly faced. And it certainly does seem to be implicit in the attitude of those who nail their flag to the mast of the market norm. For this attitude does imply that the most intelligent way for a group to use the resources at its disposal is that nobody should stand outside the matter and view the situation as a whole, and that no collective decisions should be taken in the light of any considered evaluation of the public interest; but that the collective

result should be left to emerge as the objectively determined by-product of innumerable individual decisions, from which all social considerations are, by definition, excluded. Hence it follows that those who believe that intelligence might fruitfully be directly applied to social problems (in so far as these are concerned with the wise disposal of our limited resources, in the satisfaction—be it remembered—of any need whatever, material or spiritual) should be warned off the field as dangerous trespassers. The problem of creating a satisfying and harmonious pattern of community life (for our gregarious species) thus appears as a matter in which "thinking is an idle waste of thought," if not indeed positively injurious.

(4) *If the market norm is reliable in the field in which it now operates, there is no reason to suppose that it would not be equally reliable in spheres such as the provision of fire-brigades, health services or education, from which it has in practice been ousted, in favour of some method of conscious collective decision.* Gallant upholders of the validity of the market norm generally confine their attention almost entirely to its virtues within the field in which it is, as a matter of historical experience, actually operative, and to rebutting threatened attacks upon its rule in this particular sphere. Ordinarily, the supersession of the market norm in regard to services, such as those instanced above, is tacitly condoned; while occasion-

ally such discrimination is even explicitly justified on the ground, for example, that there are certain inherently collective services which it would be patently absurd to leave in the hands of anything so individualistic as the market mechanism.

Personally, I have never been able to see the logic of this argument. Practically every service that is now provided in Western capitalist societies by collective enterprise, in flat defiance of the rulings of market demand, has at some time or place been supplied on thoroughly orthodox market principles. This is true of protection against fire, of medical services of all kinds and of education—a considerable share of the two latter services being, indeed, still regulated in England and America by strict attention to market results. Nor is the argument that there is anything inherently and peculiarly collective in these services very impressive. There are many other equally collective forms of consumption which the market daily shows itself quite well able to satisfy. In this connection, for example, it is difficult to see how provision of education differs from provision of entertainment in a cinema or theatre. Of both these services alike it may be said that they cannot be conveniently or (in market terms) economically supplied, unless large numbers of persons can be induced to consume them at the same time. In the case of the theatre this condition presents no insuperable difficulty at all, but is easily met by putting the service on the market at certain times, offering tickets of admission for sale, and regulating supply by reference to the equilibrium-point at which further tickets could only be sold at prices that make production look financially unattractive. For those who accept this market norm as a reliable indicator of what constitutes an intelligent use of resources, there does not seem to be any reason at all why the supply of education of all kinds should not be managed in an exactly similar fashion.[1]

I suggest, therefore, that defence of the market norm ought to be accompanied by much more vigorous attacks than are usually made upon those existing public services that are operated on non-commercial principles. Every successive extension of what are often called the social services is indeed ordinarily met by protests that it involves a waste of money; but these are apt to have an opportunist or political colour, instead of boldly declaring themselves as the appropriate application, in each particular instance, of a consistent and comprehensive support of the rulings of the market norm. Nor is it reasonable,

[1] The one service which really does seem to baffle the ingenuity of the market mechanism is that of defence; for no device readily suggests itself by which such of the inhabitants of a given territory as were unwilling to subscribe to the cost of maintaining an army could be prevented from enjoying its protection in time of war; or, which would adjust the amount of protection enjoyed by each citizen accurately to the amount that he chose to spend upon this service.

especially for such academic economists as have nothing to lose politically, and are still in a position to say what they please without fear or favour, to confine objection to *new* encroachments upon the sphere of "rational" or "intelligent" action in accordance with the principles of market economy. Practically the whole of our system of public education, for example ought, on these principles, to be done away with, as being a flagrant and glaringly wasteful use of scarce means; for it is plain enough that the effective demand for this service, the consumption of which is at present both heavily subsidized and to a large extent actually made obligatory, would, in a free market,[1] be quite insignificant. The equilibrium or optimum supply of education registered by the market would permit this service to absorb only a negligible fraction of the resources now devoted to it.

[1] Assuming, of course, that our existing income-structure and other economic conditions remain as at present.

Professor Robbins (*Economic Planning and International Order*, p. 254) holds that "some instruction of the young" ought to be supplied irrespective of market rulings, on the ground of "the incompatibility of contracts with infants with the principles of personal liberty." But why should not mental food for children be supplied by the market in response to their parents' effective demand in the same way as the physical sustenance and other requirements of infants are ordinarily provided (or not provided!) on market principles? As regards the education of persons who have emerged from a state of infancy, are we to infer that Professor Robbins has the courage of his faith in the market, and accepts the consequences which I have indicated under (4) above?

(5) *Strict adherence to the market norm implies that the funds now devoted to the maintenance of economists whose studies lead them to endorse this norm (as also, of course, of those who hold other opinions on this point) are wastefully employed.* The redirection of these funds to some other, strictly profitable, use would be to the public advantage. This, of course, is only a special instance of the more general argument outlined in the preceding paragraph; but it is an instance so piquant that the impulse to pick it out for specific notice could hardly be resisted. As is well known, University study is seldom self-supporting, in the commercial sense, in the modern world. The market is relatively indifferent to the services of professional economists (and of other learned men) and offers but a small effective demand for them. As things are, this melancholy[1] truth is indeed obscured by the practice of subsidizing the production of academic persons out of the taxes, or out of educational endowments; but surely those professors who uphold the ballot of the market-place should accept the verdict which it records against themselves?

[1] Melancholy, that is, to those who accept the market norm. Those who are more sceptical can better afford to laugh at it.

V

The purpose of this chapter has been to enquire how far current economic theory may justly be regarded as a system of apologetics for contemporary economic institutions—irrespective of whether the alleged apology is itself well- or ill-founded. The conclusions reached so far may be summarized as follows: (1) The concept of economy or of economical distribution of resources inevitably carries with it, at least by implication, the concept also of a norm, by which more economical may be distinguished from less economical, behaviour. (2) Since economical is virtually identical with rational behaviour (in the sense of intelligent adaptation of means to ends), few would be likely to dispute the validity of this norm in the abstract; and in fact the notion of the optimum haunts the pages even of those economists who are most anxious to keep their work strictly "positive," analysing only what is, or hypothetically might be, and who view with dismay the whole idea of economics becoming normative and dabbling in "oughts." (3) Economists will march together in defining the economic norm in some such general terms as equi-marginal returns: but the trouble really begins when we face the problem of defining "equi-marginal" in a social group. (4) An occasional economist will boldly accept actual market equilibrium as identical with the economic norm, without more ado, thus identifying the positive trends of the market with what is normatively admirable, and making himself a frank apologist for the market mechanism as it is. (5) More generally, however, the identification of market equilibrium with economic optimum is only made subject to far-reaching reservations; but (6) there is no agreement amongst economists as to just what these reservations should be, and (7) the processes of the market offer such a beautiful image of perpetual movement towards an apparent optimum that there is real danger of those reservations being forgotten in practice, and the illusory passing itself off as the substantial, optimum. As a safeguard against this and to remind the reader what urgent practical issues underlie this apparently remote philosophic discussion, I have offered some examples of the more startling consequences of complete acceptance of the market norm. Throughout the rather lengthy argument I have tried to keep continually alive a sense both of the fundamental importance of the market process, and of its essential unity, in this business of distributing our limited resources between the innumerable claims upon them. If the yardstick which the market fashions is, in fact, an accurate and reliable measure of the intelligent adaptation of means to social ends, then we have indeed an instrument of superb subtlety and delicacy; and the problem of adjusting the conflicting purposes of the various members of a social group, which looks so formidable on the surface, is hardly a problem at all. But thanks to this essential unity of *all* market relations, if this yardstick is even a little faulty in even a few places, then the *whole* of any structure built upon it is consequently modified, and the original fault is liable to be repeated and magnified indefinitely.

CHAPTER 5

ECONOMIC INDIVIDUALISM, OLD AND NEW STYLE

I

SUCH uncompromising identification of market equilibrium and economic optimum as leads to the grotesque results illustrated in the preceding chapter is, happily, not common among contemporary economists *when they are being careful to express themselves with due precision.* Those who are understood, or misunderstood (from Marshall onwards), to hold these views generally turn out to have some safeguards tucked away somewhere. Their approbation of the market is conditional, not absolute; and any fair (not to say useful) criticism of the normative significance that economists really mean to ascribe to the market must take these conditions into account.

Here we have to distinguish between two broad strands of thought, which I propose to label economic individualism of the old and new style respectively. Adherents of the old style believe that the market process has at least a potential significance as a guide to the rational distribution of resources under what is generally called a capitalist form of economic organization; while those of the new style combine great scepticism as to the validity of the market process in a capitalist society, with considerable admiration for its potentialities under socialism. It will be necessary to consider separately what kind of theoretical claims are advanced on behalf of the market by each of these schools; and to estimate both the validity of these claims, and the chances that the conditions necessary for their fulfilment can, in fact, be realized. Any of the claims that are common both to the old- and to the new-style individualists will be discussed in some detail in relation to the doctrines of the former, and only summarily mentioned when they are put forward also by the more modern school.

Now the passages already quoted reveal that there is wide disagreement between economists as to the whole range of conditions to be fulfilled if market equilibrium is correctly to interpret economic norm. The market which would satisfy one authority would be regarded as highly treacherous by another. There is, however, one stipulation which I think all would regard as vital, if normative significance is to be ascribed to the judgments of the market; viz. that the market must itself be perfectly competitive, and wholly innocent of monopolistic control. A monopolized market has its own apparatus of equilibrating tendencies, just as much as one that is competitive; but it is commonly accepted that, as long as those who enjoy monopoly powers act upon the normal market principle of putting their own economic advantage before everything else, so long will those powers, in the ordinary case,[1] be used to restrict the flow of resources into the monopolized channel to a level below that which it would reach under competition. Monopoly is essentially restrictive; and though there may be some who are prepared to identify competitive equilibrium with perfect economy, I have yet to find any who would say that a socially economical use of resources is ordinarily promoted by monopolists whose behaviour is strictly economical from their own point of view. The incidental advantages that are said sometimes to result from restriction of competition—such, for example, as greater stability—are not to be read as claims that the equilibrium of a monopolized market has anything to do with the optimum distribution of resources.

Now what are the chances of perfect competition being realized in practice?[2] No realist, I fear, would put these very high; and certainly no realist would claim that the existing markets of the contemporary world could be described as perfectly competitive. Just as we have found that the growth of monopoly

[1] The ingenious may think of exceptions to this rule; see e.g. Robinson, *Economics of Imperfect Competition*, pp. 316, 317; but its general validity will not, I think, be questioned.

[2] Aside, that is, from the "artificial" competition postulated in the socialist state of the neo-individualists. See below, pp. 211 ff.

in the modern world progressively cramps the opportunities of the economist who is interested in positive analysis,[1] so also does the same process invalidate any claim that the market can be trusted to look after the business of distributing resources in the most economical possible way. Hence those old-style individualists who put their faith in markets must also have confidence in the practicability of the actual contemporary trend towards monopoly being reversed, and a régime of pure competition being securely established in its stead. On this topic it is, for several reasons, difficult to be optimistic. For, in the first place, the advantages of combination are too plainly written on the economic field for intelligent competitors to fail to apprehend them whenever opportunity offers; second, the rapid decline of competition in the past half-century suggests that opportunity does, in fact, offer very frequently; and, third, the experience of anti-trust legislation in England and America gives little ground for hope that laws can be drafted with such close mesh that the slippery eel of monopoly cannot wriggle through them.

In the second place, every endorsement of the normative merits of the market implies (1) that the individual either knows better than anybody else what will give him satisfaction and/or (2) that he at least gets a satisfaction from the act of choosing which

[1] See above, pp. 79 ff.

outweighs any dissatisfaction that may possibly result from his making what he would himself call stupid choices; and (3) that the market offers the only, or at least the most satisfaction-giving, of all possible forms in which individuals can cooperate in choosing how resources should be distributed. All this, of course, is what Professor von Mises means when he waxes eloquent over the democratic nature of the "ballot of the market-place."

Now here we run up against a fresh set of awkward philosophical problems inherent in the concept of satisfaction itself. For how can one hope to know what satisfaction a man derives from freedom to poison himself, as compared with the slavery of having good food supplied to him without his own active co-operation in the matter? It is to be feared that the only ultimate answer to this question is that there is no answer. Each one of us may have a fairly good idea of how highly he personally rates (at its best) the privilege known as free consumer's choice; but how to compare, in an objectively satisfactory way, one man's rating of this privilege with that of another looks like being an insoluble problem. In other words, *the one thing that the market cannot measure is the satisfaction derived from its own use.* This may sound like verbal quibbling, but it is, I think, much more than that. For the strongest defence of the market is undoubtedly just that of its "democratic" character—the plea that it refers every comparison between the satisfaction-giving qualities of alternative uses of resources to a kind of popular vote. But those who put this forward as a complete and final reason for accepting market decisions as valid in all spheres are quietly begging two questions of real practical importance. First, they are begging the question of the satisfaction-giving powers of the act of choice itself. These powers they have indeed decided to rate very highly, in spite of the fact that they are, in the nature of the case, unable to check this rating by the one and only test which they themselves regard as reliably valid; viz. that of the market itself. And, second, they are begging the question of the effectiveness and accuracy of consumer-choice, as contrasted with other possible methods of enlisting public cooperation in decisions affecting the distribution of resources between alternative uses. It might, for example, be argued that the degree of freedom of choice which most of us rate highly is something at once more comprehensive and less detailed than that which the market at least affects to offer. But of this more later.[1]

As a matter of actual experience, there is indeed quite a good case to be made for the view that the market, in modern conditions, imposes upon consumers, or at least upon those of them who are even moderately affluent, a range of choice which is actually

[1] See below, pp. 191: 236; 289 ff.

burdensome. On the theory that I alone know what is satisfying to me, the market insists upon offering me a bewildering variety of alternatives from which to choose. The business of selecting between scores of varieties of cosmetics or saucepans or neckties is really very arduous, and one of which many of us would gladly be in large measure relieved. And, moreover, it is a business which most of us, most of the time, are quite incapable of conducting intelligently. True consumer's choice, with its implication of *caveat emptor*—let the buyer beware—is all very well in a society in which consumers are in general equipped at least with the minimum of technical knowledge necessary for enlightened choice. To-day, as everyone knows, they are mostly very far indeed from being in this happy state. As a purchaser of jams, for example, I am quite incapable of deciding for myself which varieties are made of fruit and which of synthetic substitutes, nor do I even know, at all accurately, how far the substitutes are, on the one hand, actively pernicious, or on the other hand, just as good as the commodity which they replace. As a purchaser of textile goods, again, I am quite incapable of discriminating between weight which is due to the quality of the material and will promote hard wearing, and the specious heaviness which is achieved by excessive loading or dressing, and which will disappear the first time that the stuff is washed or cleaned. I may, perhaps, claim to be a discriminating purchaser (discriminating, that is, of course, in terms of my own standards of satisfaction) of books on economic or sociological topics; but few of us can claim such competence in more than one or two fields. Even where we do realize our own wants and would value the power to direct resources to their satisfaction, this very readiness to exercise choice is, in fact, over and over again doomed to sterility; just because we are pathetically incapable of recognizing whether what we get is, or is not, what we wanted.

Nor is it any answer to say that in a competitive world, we can profit both by our own mistakes and by those of others, so that the more satisfying product will always, in the long run, win over the less. For, in the first place, this is an expensive and tedious way of correcting a distribution of resources which the public does not find satisfying. It is indeed true that those who have purchased material that dissolves in the wash may be to some extent forearmed next time (though, if they are still technically ignorant, even bitter experience will not be an infallible defence against a repetition of the tragedy); and true also that, in time, the boycott of an unsatisfactory product by those who have discovered its shortcomings may make its sale so unprofitable that its production is discontinued, with the result that others are spared a like experience. But this does not alter the fact that the consumer's freedom of choice would have meant a great deal more to him if he had been able to detect the faulty product *before* he had elected to buy it. And, in the second place, while suspecting that some of our choices are unsatisfactory somewhere, we may never be able, even after experience, to lay our fingers on the exact spot at which we went wrong. I want to buy good food, and I know that I may make myself and my family ill, if I fail to do so; but I may well be far too ignorant to locate just where my buying is at fault, even when I perceive that I am not getting satisfactory results.

In view of these familiar facts it is, I suggest, quite absurd to suppose that market demand can claim, even under competition, faithfully to direct resources into production of just those things that are wanted in any commonsense meaning of the word; or even to do this job so well that no alternative is worth looking at. It is far from self-evident that it would not be better, for example, in some cases to consult the consumer as to the general outline of the pattern of production, and then settle the details over his head; as a planned economic system, conducted in a politically democratic society, but not pledged rigidly to follow the lead of the market, might do. At all events for the market to establish its claim to effect the theoretically optimum distribution of resources, we have to suppose that the consumer, in addition to knowing what he wants better than anyone else, also has the power to recognize this when he gets it; and, further, that he is not irked by the incessant labour of choice that is imposed upon him. Once again the conditions which the market demands for its success look far from realistic.

II

Up to this point, however, we have ignored the stipulation, which, as we have seen, some, but not all, the economists regard as vital to the normatively correct working of the market in any sphere, viz. that there should be substantial equality of purchasing power as between consumers. Those who accept this view (and they seem to be fairly numerous from Marshall onwards) are, of course, quietly signing away *all* claims of *all* existing market valuations, at least in England and America and a great part of the rest of the world, to have any status whatever as guides to rational action. Whether the stipulation is reasonable or not is a matter that the reader must decide for himself after comparison of the classic statements on either side already referred to.[1] The answer simply turns upon the question whether one is justified in assuming that a shilling gives more satisfaction to a poor man than to a rich. On this point I would myself boldly

[1] Marshall, *Principles of Economics*, p. 471, and Robbins *Nature and Significance of Economic Science*, pp. 137–139.

assume that the verdict of common sense is plain enough—in favour of the higher satisfaction-giving power of the poor man's shilling; though admittedly the thing cannot be proved in a logically or philosophically satisfactory way, and there is no way of showing that those who find such an assumption unacceptable are wrong. But as to the *extent* of the inroads into the normative claims of the market which this assumption involves, for those who make it, there can be no two opinions. If market norms are valid only where they are not distorted by inequalities of income distribution, the kingdom over which they now reign must be Lilliputian indeed.

In short, it can hardly be denied that a market which is completely competitive, and in which there is no serious difference of income between purchasers, has a decidedly apple-pieish appearance. The more rigid of the old-style individualists, whose claims for the market are contingent upon perfect competition, and upon approximate equality of income co-existing with private ownership of capital, are certainly asking a good deal of the imagination! Experience has shown how persistent and ubiquitous is the threat of monopoly to competition, and how difficult it is to keep alive a competitive régime by any kind of artificial respiration. As to equality, *experience* has indeed less to offer; for whereas some of our modern capitalist communities have exerted themselves energetically, if none too successfully, to preserve a state of competition, none appears to have been greatly concerned about equality. And this perhaps is not unreasonable, since common-sense will here serve as well (and a great deal more cheaply) than experience. For it does not need either actual experience, or any particularly specialized training, to see that a society which depends upon the lure of the rewards of successful investment for regulating the distribution of its resources cannot afford to cancel these rewards in the interests of equality of distribution. Except in relatively backward communities, where opportunity for large aggregations of capital ownership has not yet emerged, equality of income-distribution and individualist control of capital accumulation and investment would appear to be contradictions in terms. Hence those who hold that the market's interpretation of maximum satisfaction suffers distortion wherever there is not an approximately equal income-distribution are in effect admitting that the market neither does, nor can, give sound guidance in any economic system that relies upon the profit motive to keep going.

III

The claims of the old-style individualist's market, either as it is, or as it conceivably might be, to follow the behest of the economic norm in any authoritative way begin already to look a little thin. So far, however, we have only looked at the market's ability correctly to interpret those values with which it does at least profess to deal; that is to say, at its technique for handling and compounding our conflicting evaluations of such things as cheese or mutton. But now we have to take account of a fresh set of difficulties, which arise from the fact that there are certain elements which may play an important part in influencing an individual's notions of what constitutes a satisfactory distribution of resources, but of which the market is inherently incapable of taking account.

A few examples will give an idea of the range of problems involved here. First, we have to take account of all those satisfactions which, while individually enjoyed, yet arise from the existence of a particular communal pattern of living. There is here a distinction between, on the one hand, what are sometimes called *communal satisfactions*, and, on the other hand, *individual satisfactions* arising from what the Americans would call a communal "set-up." This distinction is of the utmost importance; for the very idea of communal satisfaction, in the sense of a satisfaction enjoyed by a group as such, is meaningless to all who do not share the totalitarian conception of a group as a mystical being independent of, and additional to, the human personalities of which it is composed. For the rest of us the only living, sensitive organs capable of experiencing satisfactions, are those located in the individual minds or bodies of the individual human beings of whom any group is composed. The group, as such, has no organ in or through which sensations of satisfaction or dissatisfaction—or indeed any sensations at all—may be experienced. It is indeed the great strength of the individualists of all schools that they have clung fast to this elemental sanity of outlook in the face of all the pseudo-idealistic state- or group-worship, from Hegel to Mussolini. But to insist that only an individual can experience satisfaction is one thing: to assert that the desires of each member of a community can be, so to speak, registered, evaluated and attended to, independently of those of other members of that community, is another. And it is this second assertion which is made, on behalf of the market, by those who claim that, at least in suitable conditions of competition, etc., its mechanism is by itself capable of adequately looking after the distribution of resources in a social group.

For to adopt this attitude is automatically to rule out certain values which individuals may rate quite as highly as any of those which fall within the competence of the market. For example: one of the aspects of what I have called the "communal pattern of living," which may have great power to increase or diminish the satisfaction of individuals, is the distribution of wealth. Now the allocation of resources which is appropriate in a community, the members of which find great inequalities abhorrent, is clearly quite different from that which would reflect maximum satisfaction in a community, otherwise similar, in which contrasts of riches and poverty were, as such, regarded with indifference. But here is something with which the market is wholly unable to cope. Suppose, for example, that I am a person of substantial means, so constituted that my enjoyment of the wealth that I have acquired is gravely marred by knowledge of the distressful poverty which afflicts millions of my poorer neighbours. Now if I rely solely upon the machinery supplied by the market I am powerless to give any effect to this desire of mine for equality as such. I could, it is true, give away my fortune to the poor, in which case I should admittedly modify the inequalities which I find so disturbing—but only in a microscopic measure, since the fortune of one rich man will not go far amongst the great multitude of the poor. Social equality is an end which, in the nature of the case, I cannot attain by my own action, no matter how lavishly I may be willing to bid for it against all the myriad claims that others may be pressing upon the limited resources of the whole community. And what is true of one may be true of most, even of all, the members of the community. We might all rate social equality very high in our scales of relative valuations, and yet still, one and all, would find the market mechanism, which professes to satisfy our various wants in proportion to our own estimate of their urgency, totally incapable of giving any place at all to this important end. This mechanism will sort and weight our valuations of foreign travel, Rolls-Royces, refrigerators, cinema performances, newspapers, margarine or chewing gum, with the greatest precision;[1] but when it comes to the task of providing the kind of social environment which we find satisfying, the whole apparatus stands impotent and idle.

The example just given is merely an illustration of the fact that the market postulates a view of human nature which is atomistic to a degree that does not accord with the facts of common experience. It will hardly be disputed that we are essentially social animals; and that, in consequence, many of the values which individually we cherish most warmly are inherent in certain social patterns, and are incapable of being chopped up into the atomic individualistic mincemeat which is all that the market is able to handle. Some of our desires are so intimately bound up with the satisfaction of other people that they cannot even be recorded or their urgency assessed, unless we know how those other people are going to behave. A community, in fact, is like a party. On the one

[1] In the light, that is, of its own system of registration. "Precise weighting," in this context, is not, of course, the same thing as accurate interpretation of our actual wishes.

hand, whatever satisfactions its activities can provide are necessarily and always individually experienced, just as a successful party is enjoyed by the people who go to it, not by some mythical collectivity external to these people. And yet, on the other hand, there is a pleasure in the essentially social achievement of a successful party which is distinct from, and may even be (in the minds of the persons present) superior to, the pleasure which those same persons would derive from the pursuit of the activities that, as individualist atoms, would seem to them to offer the most satisfying way of passing the evening. Thus, some of the guests might, as atomic individuals, rate bridge-playing as preferable to dancing; others would reverse this preference; some would like conversation; others listening to music; and so on. But all might well put in front of any of these individualistic preferences the desire to co-operate in creating a happy and unified social atmosphere, in which each was aware of, and participated in, the enjoyment of all. And it is most unlikely that this result would be achieved by the method (which is the strict parallel of that employed in the economic sphere by the market) of setting the bridge players to play bridge, the dancers to dance, the conversationalists to converse, and the listeners to listen.

In actuality, this problem of evaluating and safeguarding those satisfactions which are social, in the sense that they simply disappear when atomized, is one of the most difficult of all those which face a community of human beings. Almost certainly, no group of a size larger than, say, that of the family (and mighty few even of these small communities!) can claim to have come within sight of solving it. Almost certainly, the members of, say, any political group will differ amongst themselves in their personal conceptions of what constitutes a satisfactory social pattern; and, even when they are agreed on this, it is still true that such machinery as has yet been invented for giving effect to people's wishes about the whole group picture of which they wish to form a part is extremely clumsy and ineffective. One of the worst of the difficulties is that the mere use of any machinery for this purpose may, since it almost inevitably involves a measure of compulsion, destroy one of the features of the group picture, namely freedom, which is widely and highly valued. Visualizing the kind of society in which we believe that we could be happy ourselves, we wish to assume the rôle of benevolent dictators and impose this upon our neighbours; but at the same time we think it important that our neighbours should have freedom to chose what they like, and so we fall back uneasily upon the hope that what they like is really sure to be just what we like. Here admittedly is one of the fundamental problems of adjustment of human relationships in any community which has discarded the ridiculous assumptions that all the valuation scales of every member can, even in theory, be separately listed in isolation from those of all the others; and that maximum social satisfaction can be calculated from these scales by a kind of arithmetic in which the sum of the parts is equal to the whole—that is to say in any group which takes a realistic view of the stuff of which it is composed. But a frank admission that no fully satisfactory method has been discovered, by which individual valuation of essentially social products may be included in practical interpretations of the economic norm, is no ground for complacent endorsement of the merits of a mechanism which quietly neglects these values altogether; for there is no reason whatever for supposing that the importance of these social preferences to the individual is not at least of the same order of magnitude as that of the individualistic atomic preferences which the market does attempt to reduce to a common denominator.

In the illuminating article by Mr. Durbin,[1] to which I have already referred, a number of other examples are given of preferences which may loom large in the valuation-scales of individuals, but which are incapable of being translated into the language of the market-place. These he describes as "negative preferences," represented by our willingness to pay to stop things from being produced. This category of

[1] See above, p. 81.

negative preferences marches very closely with what I have here called individual valuations of social patterns. As Mr. Durbin points out, there are probably a number of people whose satisfaction would be much enhanced if they could prevent the exhibition of a particular film, or the sale of alcoholic liquors or other products, and who would gladly pay for this satisfaction, could the opportunity to do so be made available to them. Hence the satisfaction-giving power of a product, such as a film, or a drink, must not be calculated merely by the public's willingness to pay for it in box-office or public-house, without deduction for the (unregistered) dissatisfaction which its sale causes to another section of that public. And, moreover, these negative preferences may include elements which are not merely frivolous. The desire for security, for example, is quoted as one which unquestionably stands very high in the valuation-scales of a large part of the public. But there is no way in which we can go into the market and, as it were, bid up the value of security, so as to stimulate the economic system to deliver more of this admirable product. Insecurity (of employment and investment) arises ultimately from the whimsical changeableness of recorded consumers' preferences, and a desire for security may, therefore, be regarded as a dislike, or negative preference, for excessive variability in the pattern of production. But whether it is thus described in negative terms, or, positively, as a preference for a particular kind of social pattern, there is no doubt at all either that security is, in fact, a good which is highly valued by many, or that the market mechanism is incapable of taking this valuation into account.

Finally, we must not forget that, while the market attempts to abide by its own record of our choices as between the alternatives actually offered to us, it has evolved no mechanism whatever for eliciting our opinions as to what, within the millions of possibilities, are the alternatives that we would most like to have put on offer. In other words the consumers' power of choice as between the competing uses to which resources may be put, is secondary, not primary. In practice this is a matter of the first importance. For the evidence that even the main outlines of the whole pattern of modern industrial life represent any public choosing is pretty thin. Those of us who have the means make our choice, it is true, as between Austin or Standard cars, electric or gas refrigerators, larger houses and cheaper holidays, or smaller houses and more ambitious holidays, and so on and so forth. But the really fundamental choices are made by those who decide what options to put before us. We never knew that we wanted cars and gramophones and cellophane wrappings until these things were actually produced, and we found ourselves buying them; and so to-day there may well be a myriad other commodities, which we should greatly prefer to those that we have, desire for which blooms and fades unsensed and unsatisfied by any enterprising manufacturer. Out of the incalculably wide range of our potential desires, the producer's selection of those which he proposes to exploit must be very largely a hit-and-miss affair. Nor must too much importance be attached to the obvious limitation that resources cannot long be kept in any particular use unless their product enjoys the patronage of consumers. For the effectiveness of consumer's choice is still further restricted by the fact that, in this matter of consumption, as elsewhere, one thing has a way of leading relentlessly to another. If one lives in a certain type of house (and there is only a certain number of types of house available to choose from), one is practically compelled to fill it with certain types of furnishings and gadgets (even apart from the urgency, which may itself be important, of keeping up with the Joneses); and *active* choice will have little chance to do more than select the particular brands or varieties of these furnishings and gadgets which are to be favoured. Theoretically, indeed the discriminating consumer may, by vigorous search, and by having goods made to order, compel the market to pay attention to his tastes, even when these are conspicuously different from those of his neighbours. But anyone who has experimented at all extensively along these lines knows that, in practice, such discrimination calls for qualities of perseverance and industry quite out of the ordinary. A desire that is peculiar has to have an exceptionally high degree of urgency before it is worth while facing the extra trouble necessary to make the market mechanism take notice of it. It cannot hope to compete, in the businessof distributing resources, on equal terms with demands that are more conformable to the prevailing taste. So most of us, most of the time, resign ourselves to the limitation which confines our choice to acceptance, or rejection, of proffered alternatives. These alternatives come and go, as the enterprise and imagination of manufacturers may dictate; and the whole pattern of living, the external apparatus of our civilization, undergoes corresponding changes of the profoundest sociological and psychological significance; but there is nothing to prove that the patterns which thus from time to time emerge are just those which afford maximum satisfaction to men and women whose lives conform to them.

Indeed, at the present time, such evidence as we have suggests that the characteristic forms of industrial civilization are very far from satisfying those who live under them. The decline in the reproduction rates of industrial peoples tells its tale; for it is difficult to believe that a pattern of life is satisfying—more satisfying than any imaginable alternative—when those who adopt it are everywhere found, sooner or later, unable or unwilling to reproduce their own numbers. Whether the explanation of declining fertility is itself physiological or psychological, it is sufficient criticism on any civilization that it should spell extinction for those who live under it. There must be something—and something pretty fundamental—wrong, if our ways of living are such as to inhibit our normal animal function of reproduction; and there must be something equally wrong, if our judgment of the world that we have experienced is so adverse that we are reluctant to beget children into it. It is against this background that the ultimate potency of the "free consumer's choice," which professedly shapes the forms of production according to our wishes, has to be assessed. Within the limits that the market mechanism permits (and of the only language that it can understand) we may indeed be choosing this, and rejecting that, part of the proffered picture. But at the same time, in a different, but unmistakably plain, language we are emphatically reiterating our distaste for the whole affair. Yet this protest can make no impact upon the very mechanism which boasts its unique ability to make optimum use of the opportunities afforded by life upon this planet.

Looking back then, over the whole field, we find that the market's claims to represent the true preference-scales of individuals have to be severely restricted. For those claims to be established at all, we have to swallow some pretty large assumptions such as (1) that markets are competitive; (2) that a preference for the act of choosing, and choosing in the particular form and degree made possible by the market, stands high in our valuation-scales; (3) that we are able, as well as wishful, to make intelligent choices; and (4)—in the opinion of some economists only—that there are no serious differences of wealth between the various actual and potential consumers in a given market. Further, even if and when these decidedly arduous conditions have been fulfilled, the market will still, on the one hand, blithely disregard all our essentially social valuations, along with our "negative" preferences; while, on the other hand, it necessarily confines our power of choice within a specified list of alternatives.

So much for the status of the (old-style individualist's) market as a *theoretical* optimum. Its method of pricing does, indeed, supply a subtle and ingenious instrument for measuring and comparing, *in its own terms*, certain consumer-preference-scales. And the manipulation of this instrument in economic analysis is capable, apparently, of evoking a peculiar aesthetic rapture of its own. Thus we read that "even the most blasé could scarcely resist a thrill at the exquisite delicacy of"—Samuel Bailey's exhibition of certain of Ricardo's ambiguities;[1] whilst Mr. R. F. Harrod

[1] Robbins, *Nature and Significance of Economic Science*, p. 60.

writes of the "great beauty, the exquisite workmanship" of a theoretical analysis of the—presumably tragic and sordid—problem of unemployment.[1] But all this should not blind us to the fact that aesthetic merit has nothing to do with accurate recording. The normative claims of the market in no way depend upon the opportunities that it offers for making harmonious patterns by intellectual manipulation of hypotheses in the study. These claims rest simply and solely upon the power of the mechanism *correctly* to interpret and to satisfy our wants. And on this count it is difficult to say that there is even any presumption that market equilibrium will, in practice, in any given instance, coincide with the economic norm; so that the common assumption that interference with the market process, regardless of intention or motive, will necessarily give us "the wrong industries in the wrong places"[2] is quite unjustified in the contemporary world.

It would be a mistake, however, to suppose that these conclusions dispose of every form of the old-style individualist's case. For we have still to take into account a very real distinction between a *theoretical* and a *practical* optimum. Now an economic individualist (old- or new-style) might well argue that an ideal market would offer a perfect interpretation of what, with a pardonable misuse of language, may perhaps

[1] *Economic Journal*, vol. xliv, No. 173, p. 20.
[2] See p. 160.

be called the optimum optimum. All actual markets might seem to him to be very imperfect embodiments of this ideal; but he might yet advocate, in practice, treating the critera of even these imperfect markets with as much respect as if they were perfect; on the ground that, imperfections and all, they yet offer a better guide to the solution of practical problems than any alternative *which is also practicable.* In such a case expressions of dismay at any proposal to treat market criteria with indifference or irreverence must not be taken to imply that actual markets, of themselves, realize the theoretically optimum use of resources. On the contrary, the market is merely assigned qualified approval as the practical optimum—something that is better than any available alternative.

Many of those who, like Professor von Mises or Professor Hayek, fear that disregard of the criteria of the market would lead to an irrational distribution of resources are, I suspect at heart, more concerned with the practical, than with the theoretical, optimum, even when their observations are liable to be understood as relating to theoretical comparisons. Probably they do not mean to imply anything more than: "This is far from perfect, but I cannot think of any way by which it could in practice be improved upon." Their position is comparable to that of one who wishes to obtain pieces of material of identical length and has to choose between having these measured by a yardstick of variable length or having somebody cut the stuff for him by eye. In these circumstances, a preference for the former method must not be taken necessarily to imply approval of variable yardsticks as theoretically ideal measures of length. The practical choice will clearly be determined on the one hand by the degree of variability ascribed to the yardstick, and on the other hand by the estimated competence and integrity of whoever would be responsible for the job of measuring. To drop the analogy, this simply means that one's view of the merits of the existing market mechanism as a *practical* optimum must depend upon estimates of such imponderables as the practicability of any alternative method of distributing resources in a social group; or of the compatibility of possible alternatives with freedom or democracy or other social concepts that may be highly valued. These are vast questions that it is impossible to discuss fully here. Two comments, however, seem to be apt at this point. First, I must record that, for my own part, when I review the evidence of under-nourishment, miserable housing and lack of the amenities of civilized living generally, alongside of sybaritic luxury, which obtrude themselves upon the notice of any casual observer in any great city of most of Europe and America, I find it difficult to convince myself that we really could not, if we cared to try, distribute our resources in a way which would give greater aggregate satisfaction than this. Second, in the particular context of this essay, the question whether market processes are to be regarded as indicating theoretical or merely practical optima, in the sense in which these terms are here used, is by no means one which economists, as students of market processes, can afford to treat with indifference. It has, indeed, a very direct bearing upon their own future. For if it should be admitted that the market is, and always must be, a distorted and imperfect embodiment of the economic norm, then it would be inevitable and proper that interest should shift away from the market and all its works towards the possibility of improving upon the known alternatives to it. For the prolonged study (even from the positive angle) of a method of distributing resources which is convicted of always distributing them badly is not a pastime to which minds that are blessed with a sense of practical responsibility will happily betake themselves.[1]

IV

We have now to consider the potential claims of the market as set out by those whom I have described as the neo-individualists—that is, those who picture a society in which all industry is "socialized" and there is no private ownership of capital; but in which the socialized enterprises, as has been aptly said "play at

[1] See also below, p. 246.

competition,"[1] faithfully following the laws of the market, even though the spur of personal economic gain no longer compels their managers to do so. This, in the long established sense of the word, is, of course, a form of socialism. But to describe such an economic system as a "planned society," as is sometimes done, is to invite confusion. "Planning," in ordinary speech, suggests a deliberate review of the elements of any situation, followed by conscious execution of policies that are themselves consciously and deliberately selected, in the light of this review. It is, however, as we have already seen, the characteristic feature of any market economy that it evades the necessity for any *conscious* and *deliberate* review of the problem of allocating resources between competing uses in a social group; and that, instead, it allows the social pattern to emerge as the result of the market's responses to millions of uncoordinated stimuli, arising from the demands of individuals. While a case can be made (as old- or new-style individualists from Adam Smith to Abram Lerner[2] claim) for the view that, in suitable conditions, the resulting social pattern will be harmonious, and may even be the closest possible approximation to the economic norm, it is none the less an odd use of words to describe this process as "planning." Indeed, the strongest arguments usually

[1] Robbins, *Economic Planning and International Order*, p. 208.

[2] See footnote to p. 216.

adduced in support of the market as an instrument for allocating resources are just those of its flexibility and capacity to adapt itself at all times to the most unexpected demands from all quarters—a readiness, in fact, to run from one course to another, which is just the opposite of the steady, purposive consistency associated with ruthless adherence to a preconceived plan. A man who, on returning to work from his summer holiday, plans to visit Czecho-Slovakia the following year, and, in accordance with this project, spends his winter leisure in studying Czech history and culture, and who then books his ticket and hotel accommodation well in advance of the date of departure, might reasonably be called a planner; but one who did not decide where to spend his vacation till the last minute, so that he might have the latest news about the weather, the rates of exchange and the political situation before committing himself, or who set out to go to Czecho-Slovakia but changed his mind half-way and went to Greece instead, would hardly be called a planner in the same sense.

Since every market economy, socialist or capitalist, conforms much more closely to the latter than to the former analogy, I propose to confine the term "planned" to those cases in which resources are *deliberately* (whether by dictator, elected Parliament, ministerial order or any other means) distributed in a certain way; or in which the market mechanism is *deliberately* manipulated (as by subsidies or differential taxes) with the object of producing a pattern other than that which would have resulted from its own spontaneous activity; or in which the market survives as servant rather than master, as when public authorities holding a monopoly of supplies are in a position to fix prices authoritatively in the way that suits their preconceived purposes.[1] This is only a matter of terminology, but it is conducive to clear thinking to adopt a terminology which is, as far as possible, in harmony with current usage.

We are thus able to distinguish three possible types of economic system:[2] namely the capitalist market economy; the socialist market economy; and the socialist planned economy. All existing economic systems are, of course, hybrids containing elements of all these three types; but, roughly speaking, we may regard contemporary England and the United States of America as approximating most closely to the first type; the Soviet Union as a compound of the second and third; Nazi Germany as a compound chiefly of the first and third; while the neo-individualism, which

[1] As long as any "free" market remains anywhere, in which consumers are at liberty to buy or not to buy, no authority can, of course, regard the market as a completely passive tool in his hands; but there is a world of difference between acceptance of the market's domination (economic individualism, old- or new-style) and confining market forces within the strait-jacket of planned objectives.

[2] These do not, of course, exhaust the theoretical possibilities.

is of special interest from the point of view of this essay, is a relatively pure but hitherto unrealized specimen of the second variety.

Now the important thing about this hypothetical socialist market economy is that, generally speaking, it accepts the rule of the market. In such a régime goods are produced and offered for sale in a market; but their production is carried on by socialized enterprises, the capital of which is owned by a public body (like the capital of, say, a municipal gas-works in our own country), with the result that no single person is interested as profit- or interest-receiver in the results of any particular one of these enterprises. In all other respects, however, every socialized enterprise behaves as though it were a textbook example of a profit-seeking unit in a *competitive* capitalist world. For example, one group of enterprises is making television sets: another electric refrigerators. If the market demand for these two commodities turns out to be such that the television sets are almost unsalable at a price covering their money cost of production, while the refrigerators sell like wildfire, the refrigerator enterprises will be making handsome profits, while the television industry will show little or none. This will be equivalent to an instruction to the managers of the refrigerator works to increase production; and for this purpose their managers will, so to speak, go into the labour market and bid competitively for more labour, offering better wages or conditions as an inducement to workers to enter this particular line of employment; and in just the same way additional capital will "flow" into refrigerator manufacture, attracted by the higher profit obtainable there, even though it will not be impelled thither by the acquisitive instincts of greedy capitalists; and all this will continue (along, of course, with a reverse process in the television industry) up to the point at which equilibrium is restored by the equalization of the return to capital in both fields. This, in briefest outline, is what is meant by "playing at competition."

The image of some such world as this has, of recent years, been much before the eyes of those socialists who have been well-trained in the modern derivatives of classical English economics; and the whole matter has been, and still is, the subject of lively controversy. The question posed has, however, more often been: "Could a socialist state follow the market?" rather than "should it do so?"; whereas it is primarily the latter that concerns us here. Since, however, there is no purpose in discussing the wisdom of a course which turns out to be impossible, a few words must be said here to establish at least a presumption of the practicability of the socialist market economy.[1]

[1] The reader who wishes to see this topic more adequately treated should refer to the essays in *Collectivist Economic Planning* (edited by Professor Hayek); to the controversy between Mr.

For this purpose a further distinction must be made between two alternative distinct forms of such an economy. In the first,[1] the socialized enterprises seek to imitate competitive textbook individualism as nearly as possible in every respect, bar the one which is ruled out by the very fact that they *are* socialized. As implied in the example just given, the production of goods is, in this case, regulated by realized profits, labour is attracted from this employment to that by the lure of higher wages, and capital is assigned to whatever enterprise can afford to bid highest for its use. The labour market, and also the market for consumption goods, as we know them, are preserved almost unchanged, adjustments in employment and in consumption being brought about by the spontaneous, uncoordinated reactions of individuals to the opportunities offered to them; while the market for investment is replaced by a lifelike imitation of the original, in which socialized enterprises model their behaviour upon that of the competing capitalists whom they have ousted.

One important limitation upon the rule of the market in such a society cannot, however, be avoided, namely, that the socialist state is compelled to decide

Dobb, Mr. Lange and Mr. Lerner in the *Review of Economic Studies*, vol. ii, Nos. 2 and 3, vol. iv, Nos. 1 and 2; and to articles by Messrs. Dobb and Dickinson in the *Economic Journal*, vol. xliii, Nos. 170, 172 and 173.

[1] For discussion of the second, see pp. 227 ff.

by deliberate planning—that is without recourse to any market—the proportion of current income that is to be set aside or saved, in order to augment the capital of the future;[1] for where there is no private ownership of capital there are, by definition, no private owners able to settle for themselves, according to the rules of the market, what proportion of their incomes shall be invested rather than spent. When nobody has any opportunity whatever to become an investor, obviously nobody will have to decide how much he thinks it worth while to invest. But even this difference between the socialist and the capitalist market economy is less significant than might at first be thought; for although, in a capitalist society, the decision how much current income is to be spent and how much saved and invested (i.e. how the community's resources are to be allocated as between the production of consumable goods and of new capital equipment) is left to the public to make as it pleases, yet it is now generally agreed that in this matter the public's behaviour is apt to be somewhat incalculable and not at all neatly conformable to market principles. In other words the saving and investing business by which capital is created (as distinct from distributed

[1] Or, to be more precise, the socialist state must decide *either* the amount of capital to be invested, *or* the rate of profit to be realized by the socialized enterprises. See the article by Mr. Dickinson already referred to, *Economic Journal*, vol. xliii, No. 170.

between alternative uses), is, even as things are, largely a matter of convention and habit and mood, rather than of nice adjustment to the price offered for the job. Everybody knows that it is far from certain that a rise in the current rate of interest from 5 to 6 per cent will induce those who are in a position to do so to scrape together additional savings so as to take advantage of the extra percentage;[1] though, of course, there is practically no doubt at all that, of two otherwise similar investments, the one which offers 6 per cent will be more successful in attracting capital, than that which can promise only 5 per cent. Hence, the fact that a socialist market economy can get no guidance from the market in deciding how much of the revenue of the various socialized enterprises is to be set aside for future development, does not, after all, make it so very different from a market economy in which capital is private property, and is dissipated by the spendthrift, or piled up by the miser, according to their several tastes and temperaments.

A second limitation upon strict adherence to market norms in the socialist market economy arises in the business of estimating risk. In the world that we know this problem is referred to the judgment of

[1] Especially now that saving is so largely in the hands of joint stock companies and other corporate bodies, on which matter see the striking evidence collected in Clark, *National Income and Outlay*, chapter viii.

individual investors, which judgments are compounded together on strictly market principles. Thus, on the average over a period, a speculative project is expected to yield a higher return than one which is as secure as the Bank of England; for if it cannot give at least plausible promises of ability to do so, people will be reluctant to invest in it, and the whole proposition may have to be abandoned, the market having voted that it is not worth going on with. Further (which is important) the exact *amount* of extra return necessary to compensate for any and every degree of risk is itself settled by this market process of trial and error. An apparently madcap scheme must offer 20 per cent or more, while other flotations, of slightly more sober appearance, may look equally as attractive on a promise of only 15 per cent.

In the socialist market economy, however, this process is ruled out, since again there are no capitalists to weigh with nicety the exact amount of anguish caused by the prospect of dividends occasionally being passed, or the exact amount of payment necessary to compensate for this suffering. The managers of the socialized enterprises (or those who give them their instructions) have to estimate the community's willingness to face risks *vicariously*; whereas it is of the essence of market decisions that he who pays the piper calls the tune, and that production and investment in every case must follow the instructions (as recorded in the market) of the consumers and investors directly concerned, or their nominees, and not those of some superior person who claims to "plan" on their behalf. In the socialist market economy, if capital is invested in the production of, say, synthetic wool, and this product turns out to be a failure, which the consuming public refuses to buy, the resulting loss cannot be brought home to just those persons who are rash enough to put their capital into this particular venture. The socialized Synthetic Wool Corporation will, it is true, be liquidated on orthodox market principles, *after* this failure has been experienced, and will thus be prevented from bidding for further capital; but the wisdom or unwisdom of the original decision to establish such an enterprise cannot be referred to any "ballot of the market-place." It must be essentially a planned, as distinct from a market, decision. On this account the decisions about the distribution of capital that result from play-competition in the socialized market economy will be unlikely to be identical with those which a market of real flesh-and-blood self-interested capitalists would make; and *on the theory that the market is always right*, these decisions may, in consequence, be wrong decisions.

With these exceptions, however, it does appear that there is nothing inherently impossible in playing at competition. The socialized market economy will, I think, have to recognize that, at the points named, there must be a blank in the instructions received from the market. But, in other respects, the fact that the capital of all enterprises is public property should not prevent the managers of those enterprises from behaving as though they were employed by the most zealously acquisitive private shareholders—that is to say if they choose, or are under orders, so to behave. Indeed, from this point of view the fact that capital is public property appears to be irrelevant. Just as the principles of commercial management remain the same, and can be equally well followed, whether the capital of a concern is held by dukes or dustmen, insurance companies or trade unions, so also it would seem, will those principles remain unchanged, should that capital be acquired by state or municipality, and private shareholders be eliminated altogether.

I shall, therefore, assume that the impossibility of "playing at competition" is, at the least, not proven; and that it is, accordingly, worth while exploring the question, with which this essay is more directly concerned, of the potential normative significance of the market in a socialized market economy. Here, I think, even quite superficial reflection does suggest that some at least of the criticisms, which have been made above upon the validity of market norms in a capitalist society, might very well be ruled out if the private ownership of capital were eliminated, and all socialized enterprises were to follow the rules of textbook competition faithfully to the letter. For, in the first place, whereas it is common experience that competition-in-earnest has a tendency to end in the monopolistic combination of the competitors, play-competition must, by definition, remain competitive. And the difficulties which have frustrated efforts artificially to maintain competition under capitalism would hardly arise in the same form in a socialized economy. For if we suppose that any such socialist society is able to make its officials obey any instruction at all (and if it could not do this, it could not, of course, survive for a day) there is no reason why those who are placed in charge of its socialized enterprises should have any special reluctance to conform to the particular policy of conducting their business on strictly commercial lines, while at the same time eschewing the peculiar opportunities of profit offered by monopolistic combination. When these managers no longer have any personal financial interest in the revenues of the enterprises over which they preside, the instruction not to exploit the possibilities of monopoly ceases to be equivalent to a demand that they should renounce attractive opportunities of personal enrichment. It might, of course, happen that the play-competition of a socialist economy would be relatively inert as compared with that of genuinely competitive capitalism. The manager of a socialized enterprise might be just disinclined to take the trouble always to introduce new methods and improvements as they came to his notice; whereas a capitalist competitor, who scents a possible fortune in such changes, will naturally hurry to be the first to take advantage of them. And further, since, in the socialized market economy, any manager who is particularly energetic in putting into effect the latest improvements in technique and organization will be likely to take custom and profit away from his fellows, and so bring them into bad odour with the authorities (and perhaps even endanger the future of their enterprises and their jobs), it might even happen that the managers generally would be tempted secretly to get together and persuade any over-enterprising colleague to damp down his ardour. In these and other ways it is easy to foresee that the edge of competition might be blunted in a socialized economy, unless very clever and vigorous measures were taken to prevent this. But it still remains true that the peculiar and powerful incentive which in a capitalist society is continually impelling competition to liquidate itself in monopoly is only operative so long as capital is privately owned, and there are pockets waiting to be lined by monopoly gains.

In the second place, it is not unreasonable to suppose that perversion of the consumer's judgment, either by ignorance, or by misrepresentation on the part of those from whom he buys, would be much less serious in a socialized economy. This is indeed one of the oldest arguments in favour of their projects used by socialists of all kinds. In the world that we know every seller has a direct financial interest in making us buy *his* product, and buy it from *him*; and it is, of course, to this end that all the arts of modern salesmanship are directed. In a socialized economy this direct financial incentive to harry and bamboozle the unfortunate consumer is removed, and it is thus made much easier for advertisement to be redirected to its proper business of giving the consumer such accurate information as will assist him to realize his own preferences, and lighten the burden of his choice, instead of, as too often happens at present, actually obstructing his wishes and aggravating that burden. Even if it be admitted that motives of prestige may still induce the representatives of the various socialized enterprises on occasion to employ somewhat dubious wiles in their competition for custom, this does not alter the fact that prestige alone is a much less powerful incentive than the compound of prestige *plus* financial interest which motivates the present salesmanship of capitalist enterprises.

Third, those economists who believe that existing market processes are distorted by inequalities in the distribution of wealth and income can take a much more hopeful view of the normative significance of market readings in a socialized economy.[1] For the most glaring and obstinate inequalities of wealth are due to ownership of property rather than to inequality of earning power. In a socialized society where there are no capitalists, obviously there are no rich capitalists; and with very few exceptions, the spread between rich and poor is likely to be very much less than it is with us. In these circumstances, if it is found that greater profits are derived from the sale of *marrons glacés* than of milk, it may reasonably be concluded that the former are at the moment satisfying a more urgently felt public need than the latter; and we no longer have to reckon with the possibility that unsatisfied desires for milk are left out of account because of the poverty of those who experience them.

It is not, however, claimed by anybody that the elimination of private ownership of capital would, by itself, *completely* resolve *all* differences in income. Unless indeed everybody was willing and able to do everybody else's job (and to do it at a moment's notice), there could not possibly be absolute equality of income in any economy in which labour was bought and sold on market principles. The large incomes, for example, commanded by gifted entertainers and authors, so charmingly designated by

[1] See above, p. 192.

Marshall the "rents of rare natural ability," will remain large, so long as the abilities for which they are paid remain both rare and natural (as distinct from acquired), and continue to appeal to popular demands. It is as plain as a pikestaff that, even if a socialist society greatly extended the opportunities for all and sundry to acquire any and every kind of skill, and took all possible steps to facilitate the movement from place to place, and from job to job, of any workers who had an interest in moving, there would still be occupations in which a relative scarcity of labour resulted in exceptionally high wages, as also would there be others in which too many cooks would lower the pay. Indeed a labour market *can* only fulfil its proper function of allocating workers to different industries according to the various demands for their services, in so far as it can manipulate wages up and down—that is to say, in so far as it is free to override any canon of equal pay for all.

In consequence of this limitation those who attach great importance to strict equality of income, either for its own sake, or because they believe that the only reliable interpretation of the economic norm is that provided by a market mechanism which is not distorted by inequalities of consumer-purchasing power, have suggested an alternative form of socialist market economy in which an imaginary labour market (as well as an imaginary capital market) is, as it were, substituted for a real one. Under this ingenious proposal, the actual payments made to workers are wholly divorced from the market value of the work done. All are paid the same wage; or, if differences are permitted, these are based upon variations in the recipient's needs (a family man perhaps being paid more than a bachelor), rather than upon variations in performance, or in the public demand for different types of labour. This applies, that is to say, to the wages that are *actually* paid. But the payments that appear in the books of any socialized enterprise, and so determine the appearance of its profit-and-loss account, and through this its success in the play-competition with other enterprises for capital, are quite differently calculated. This is where our imaginary labour market comes in. For each enterprise reckons its labour costs for accounting purposes at the figure which it *would* have had to pay, if there had been a real labour market, and if it had been buying labour on orthodox commercial principles. In other words, it is the market value of a man's labour which in every case is entered in the books of his socialist employers, and plays its part in determining the distribution of his scarce labour in accordance with market demand; and yet there is nothing in his pay envelope to indicate what that market value may be.

This ingenious combination of equalitarianism

with strict obedience to the rule of the market is certainly very attractive; but it is to be expected that practical difficulties will begin to pile up when *both* the labour *and* the capital markets are imaginary. Mr. Dickinson,[1] who has proposed such an economy, does not think that the necessary accounting would involve insoluble problems. He does, however, point out that such a system would "add to the complexity of book-keeping," and that, if people were still allowed to choose what occupation they would follow, it would play havoc with the distribution of labour. Any final judgment as to whether the whole scheme must be pronounced inherently impracticable, on the ground that it would be impossible to get from imaginary markets the essential data supplied by real ones, turns largely upon considerations that are too technical to be discussed in detail here. It may, however, be worth pointing out that this business of imputing value to a particular use of labour or capital will be *more* than twice as difficult when there is neither a capital nor a labour market, as when one or other of these survives in actuality. An example may help to show this. Thus, let us suppose that an exceptionally high rate of profit is realized by the group of socialized enterprises which are engaged in the production of typewriters. This simply means that the market is for the time being ascribing a higher

[1] *Economic Journal*, vol. xliii, No. 170.

value to capital and labour when these are devoted to the making of typewriters, than when they are otherwise used; and that accordingly a presumptive case is made out for expansion in the typewriter industry. But how is this higher value to be distributed as between typewriter mechanics and typewriter capital? If there were *either* a real labour market *or* a real capital market this question would (theoretically anyhow!) settle itself by ordinary market processes, since whichever factor was still actually bought or sold would extract its share of the increased value by ordinary market bargaining; and it might then be presumed that whatever remained was to be credited to the other factor, the market for which was only imaginary. Thus, if we suppose that the market for labour is retained, then, in the circumstances postulated, the typewriter mechanics would be in a position to demand higher wages; and the number of additional workers who would "flow" into the industry would settle itself by the measure in which these higher wages induced people in other occupations to seek employment in the typewriter business. The higher labour costs would thus be ascertained by experience, and the increased return to capital invested in typewriter manufacture would be inferred by deducting these costs (and of course any other increased charges similarly experienced) from the gross revenue paid by the eager buyers of typewriters. But one cannot solve the simple equation $x = y - z$ if one does not know the value of z as well as of y.

Moreover, the situation is further complicated by the fact that in real life it is very unlikely that there will not be alternative ways of producing type-writers, some of which involve the use of a relatively high proportion of labour and less machinery, while others require less labour and more machinery. It is not easy to see how a socialist economy is to decide between such alternatives on strictly market principles, when there is no flesh-and-blood market *either* for labour *or* for capital to which the issue can be referred. And on top of all this we have to remember that, just as the capitalist has more to think of than the mere rate of interest offered in deciding what to do with his capital, so the worker has more to think of than the mere rate of money wages in deciding what profession he elects to follow. In discussing the distribution of capital between different industries in a socialist market economy, we found that it would not be easy to assess just how much of the profits of a particularly speculative enterprise ought to be ear-marked as compensation for the risk that the thing may turn out to be a failure, and the capital invested in it presently earn no profits at all; since, in such an economy, the present method of referring the matter to the "ballot-box of the capital market" and settling it there is no longer practicable. In exactly the same way, it is going to be a very tricky matter for the socialized economy to determine just what valuation is to be put upon such factors as monotony, risk of injury, chances of promotion or hours of work, all of which are ordinarily taken into account quite as much as mere money wages, by workers who are intelligently debating the merits of alternative openings. Just as the capitalists in a non-socialized world register their own estimation of degrees of risk through the capital market, so also in that world does estimation of the incidental advantages and disadvantages of various *occupations* stand referred to the judgment of the persons concerned, as recorded by the market in which they sell their labour. Substitute a hypothetical for a real labour market in either case, and the basis of calculation is destroyed.

On such counts as these, it seems to me very improbable that a socialized market economy would be able *both* religiously to follow the rule of the market in its distribution of resources, *and* to pay for work done on equalitarian principles. In practice that measure of inequality of consumer-purchasing-power which arises from inequality in earning power (i.e. in ability immediately to supply the services for which the public is most ready to pay) would probably have to be winked at in a socialist market economy; and the labour of human beings would still have to be treated, in daily life, as well as in the mysteries of socialist book-keeping, as "merchandise or an article of commerce." Inevitably this would mean that some inequalities would remain, and that certain consumers would therefore enjoy the privilege of wielding plural votes in the ballot of the market-place. These inequalities would, however, certainly be far less conspicuous than those that are associated with the private ownership of invested capital.

V

All in all, then, it appears that the claim of the markets of the socialist market economy to interpret the economic norm are superior, in several noteworthy particulars, to those of the markets of capitalism. It remains only to consider what reservations would still have to be made before, even in a socialized economy market, equilibrium could be wholeheartedly identified with "optimum"; and what is the bearing of those limitations upon the scope of the topics to which students of economics may most usefully address themselves.

If the reader will now recall the argument of pages 184-206 he will, I think, agree that, socialism or no socialism, we must still exercise some caution in accepting the market version of what constitutes an optimum distribution of resources. For among the criticisms of the market there propounded there still remain some (and some of the most radical, too) that are just as much applicable to the markets of a socialized economy as to those of capitalism. In particular, it would be just as true in a socialist as in a capitalist society, that the market mechanism could offer us no opportunity of registering our approval or disapproval of that mechanism itself. All the arguments would still be valid which suggest that the extra satisfaction, which consumers derive from the power of nicely regulating through the market the quantity of resources devoted to a particular use, is on occasion simply not worth the effort involved in the exercise of that power. As has been suggested in these pages before,[1] the right of choice can be an affliction just as much as a privilege; and it is in all seriousness likely to be an affliction, and to be undervalued where it might be a real privilege, if we are compelled too often to exercise it upon frivolous or insignificant occasions.

As a matter of practical politics it seems to me grossly improbable that any socialist society would accept the market's judgment as to the optimum distribution of resources in *all* fields. Rightly or wrongly I cannot help thinking that it would be sure to subsidize, among other things, health and educational services. And it seems equally probable that a social-

[1] See pp. 188, 189.

ized economy would follow the common practice of capitalism in supplying water on completely communistic, or "planned" principles, thus wholly relieving consumers of the pleasure or burden (whichever it is) of regulating supply by market demand. There would, however, be no objective market criterion by which our socialists could justify their decision thus to scrap the market in these particular instances; and equally would there be no objective criterion by which they could be guided in settling whether or no this violation of market rules should be extended also to other fields, and such things as salt, or bread, or soap, "laid on" like water. If the case for the market is not proven in regard to water, it is neither more nor less *proven* in these other instances. The doctrine that the market is always right, that production should follow competitive profit, may or may not be sound. But it is equally true, both in a socialist and in a capitalist economy, that its soundness cannot itself be tested in any market. It is a matter upon which we have to make up our minds, consciously, and in the light of quite general considerations; and our composite answer has to be worked out, in every case, by a crude and fumbling process, unaided by reliance upon the objective record of profit and loss accounts.

Second, it must, of course, be as true under socialism as under capitalism that the market cannot, as a rule, offer a more active choice than the right to say "yes" or "no"—"more" or "less"—to the particular products set before us. In a socialist society, just as much as in one that is served by private enterprise, production will almost always have to be carried on in anticipation of demand; and, in consequence, all conceivable alternative uses of resources, except those with which producers happen to decide to experiment, will be outside the purview of the market altogether. An intelligent socialist society might indeed rack its brains very energetically over the problem of giving the public at large more initiative in determining the general way of life which is agreeable to them. It might, as it were, sketch broad alternative programmes and try to elicit opinions, informed, and uninformed, about them. Certainly it would not be easy to find a way of doing this that would be constructively useful; but the one thing that is quite clear is that the issues which are referred to the *market* ballot must themselves still be subjected to a prior selection, in which this ballot has no part.

Third, there is nothing to enable a socialized market to take account of so-called negative preferences. The consumer would still be able, in the socialist market economy, as now, to signify his distaste for certain products by quietly refusing to buy them; but he would be in no better position to make his preference effective, should he wish to go further, and actually be prepared to pay a price in order to stop the supply of commodities the production of which, for one reason or another, fills him with dismay.

Now it will be remembered that one of the most likely reasons (apart from Mrs. Grundyism) for wishing to obstruct the diversion of resources to new uses is a fear of the insecurity which is begotten of extreme changeableness. Often we would rather have security than variety, but the market does not give us any opportunity of saying so. But here is something which a socialist society could surely ill afford to ignore; for the insecurity of life under capitalism, and the heavy mental and material toll taken by unemployment, have always been some of the factors most potent in breeding socialists. Indeed there are few arguments in support of a planned society more popular than the belief that it would, or anyhow could, abolish unemployment. Nor, I think, is this belief illusory. I have outlined elsewhere the main reasons for thinking that a planned society (using the word in the sense indicated above[1]), could virtually eliminate unemployment, *provided that it set this aim in front of all others.*[2] Here perhaps it will suffice to put the matter in a very extreme form by recalling that there is never any problem of unemployment in any group in which the market has been eliminated

[1] See p. 212. [2] *Plan or No Plan*, pp. 205–209.

altogether: such, for example, as a monastery or an army. In such communities as these the distribution of time and resources may indeed be very wastefully managed; but no one ever suffers from wanting work and being unable to find it.

Now the more completely planned is the economic life of any community, the more does it approximate, in this particular respect, to a monastery or an army; and the more credible, accordingly, is its claim that it could find work for all its members. This claim, to be sure, can only be substantiated if the managers of the planned economy think it so important for a man to be at work in some form or other that they are prepared, if necessary, to disregard the question whether his work is, in any ordinary sense, remunerative; whether, that is, it will pay for his keep. That is what was meant above by the statement that a socialist planned economy could abolish unemployment, *provided that it set this aim before all others*. Of course such a policy is open to the criticism that it is ridiculous to set people to work digging holes and filling them up again, or performing those tasks which are the more subtle modern equivalent of this exercise—boondoggling, as the Americans would so expressively describe it. The planned economy's answer to this criticism would, however, take the form of posing the question; when is a boondoggle not a boondoggle? or (in European English) by what test can one diagnose the difference between digging a hole that is to be filled up again, and digging one that is wanted? And this is not as silly as it sounds. For the critic is inevitably driven back on the market as his only available criterion, and can only reply that work is unremunerative when it does not show a profit on the basis of market demand and market cost. Those, however, who are dubious, in the light of the argument of this chapter, of the infallibility of the market's idea of the optimum will not be willing uncritically to accept this verdict. They may very well urge that there are occasions, when the employment of resources on lines of production that will not sell for a profit, gives a result that is actually much nearer the optimum than the alternative which would be realized if the market were left to have its way. In particular, they will certainly remind the critics that the market is wholly indifferent to the very real satisfaction derived from security, or from the mere fact of having a job at all; and that it is just because their policies take account of these important values that they claim to be interpreting the optimum more intelligently.

All this is equivalent to saying that a socialist society which proposes to follow the market as faithfully as it can will have to be extremely guarded in the claims that it makes about doing away with unemployment. Unemployment is essentially the result of imperfect adjustment to market change. By facilitating the movement of labour, and by doing away with monopolistic restrictions of all kinds, a socialist market economy could, no doubt, materially reduce the duration of periods of transition from one market equilibrium-point to another; but in so far as it is pledged to follow the market's whims, it cannot hope entirely to evade the consequences of those whims. Declining demand in any industry will mean both reductions of wages and dismissals of workers; and unless they have made quite astonishing progress in educating the public in economic orthodoxy, the managers of socialized enterprises which are discharging labour must expect to hear bitter criticism of an economic system in which men and women suffer unemployment just because a profit cannot be made out of their labour. It will certainly be a tough job to accustom the mind of the socialist rank and file to the idea that, under socialism also, production is for profit and not for use. I do not say that this job may not have to be undertaken; but if it has, there is much to be said for getting to work on it now, so that the public may have the widest possible understanding of what is to be expected.

Naturally the price to be paid, in terms of insecurity, for rigid aherence to market canons will, in large measure, depend upon the degree to which the socialist society that we are visualizing engages in trade with the rest of the world. In the extreme case in which our socialists are living in a wholly closed community, there would be comparatively little to fear from the vagaries of the market; especially as, as we have seen, the decision to try out a new product must of necessity be a planned decision, not itself emanating from any market. In such a case the authorities could, for example, adopt a go-slow policy in tickling our appetites with new gadgets and new entertainments; though if the play-competition between the socialized enterprises is to be at all realistic, they could hardly also justify a similar policy of ca' canny in the introduction of improved technical methods of production, which are apt to be just as fertile sources of market instability as are changes in consumer-demands. Further they could probably indulge in some philosophical equivocation in determining what constitutes "really free" choice, and employ the arts of advertisement so as to discourage excessive variability in consumption. But all this becomes enormously much more difficult in a community which is accustomed to trade extensively with other countries, and which cannot forego its foreign trade without very severe sacrifice. As everybody knows, it is the vagaries of foreign demand which, in the main, have brought the British coal and cotton industries to their present pass. A socialist market economy in Britain, which stuck to the principle that it is improper to permit workers to be employed except when their employment yields commercial profit, would surely find these principles severely strained by any situation like that which has brought our miners, shipbuilders and textile operatives to their present plight.

VI

Analysis of the normative significance of the market in either a capitalist or a socialist society thus reveals that it is, in *all* circumstances, very imprudent uncritically to endorse market equilibrium as a reliable interpretation of the optimum way of using our scarce means. If we do so, we are almost certain, on occasion, to arrive at results which are repugnant to horse-sense; and there are solid reasons why this should be so. Owing, however, to the common tendency to assume that, if one extreme position is found to be untenable, its opposite is thereby established as beyond criticism, it may be useful to point out here just what the conclusions of this chapter do *not* mean. They do *not* mean that market decisions are completely meaningless and ought in all circumstances to be disregarded entirely. Market demand is a guide of a sort, sometimes more, sometimes less, reliable—more, I think, in a socialized economy, than in one where capital is privately owned. It is just not anywhere infallible, that is all; and any argument which sets out from the premise of market infallibility will reach a vicious conclusion.

It is just this qualified, half-and-half view of the market which has a vital bearing upon the problem of directing economic enquiry into channels where it will not be stultified, or deservedly ridiculous. That topic, however, is large enough to demand a chapter to itself.

CHAPTER 6

TOWARDS A NEW FOUNDATION

I

THE position at which we have now arrived may be summarized as follows. The modern analytical economist is concerned with human behaviour in the distribution of scarce means between alternative uses, in so far as this behaviour is exhibited in the activities of the market. All these market processes have a certain unity, inasmuch as all are obedient to one or other of the manifestations of the same guiding principle—that is, the principle of economy or of equi-marginal returns. The economist does not concern himself with the merits and demerits, nor even with the whys and the wherefores, of the purposes which appear in the market as ends. It is of no interest to him to enquire why women now habitually pay substantial sums of money to have their hair permanently waved, whereas twenty years ago they saved their money and went about (in this respect) as Nature intended that they should; but he is, on the other hand, very deeply engrossed in observation of the complex and delicate mechanism by which just so much and no more of the resources of society have been converted into the shop-premises, machines, electrical supplies and operative skill necessary to satisfy this new demand. At the same time, we found that—if only because the principle of economy itself is so obviously common-sensical—it is very difficult, even for those economists who wish to do so, to divest their discussions completely of all normative significance. The market is always straining after something which appears to it—or rather to the people in it—as an optimum. Not unnaturally, the economist who, as it were, walks about the market-place all day long, observing the goings-on there, is also liable to slip into the habit of talking in terms of this same optimum and of endorsing its optimal character. Sometimes he blesses the norms of the market with his express approval: sometimes his endorsement is implicit: and sometimes he sticks more rigidly to his professed business, and expressly affirms that market norms are valid only *within a given system of preference-scales, as those scales are themselves recorded in the market's own notation.*

As soon, however, as we permitted ourselves to stand right outside the market, and made an attempt to assess the accuracy of its mechanism for interpreting and weighing the competing claims of the members of a social group, grave doubts began to arise as to its ability to make a reasonably good and comprehensive job of its own business. At the best, the market does not look like being able to cover more than a part of the field. There are certain ends which cannot, by their very nature, be reduced to the peculiar, atomic form, which alone is tractable by its methods. And at the worst (which means in practice, especially where there is great inequality, very often), it requires a large stretch of the imagination to acquit the market of actually falsifying and misreading those ends which do come within its sphere.

Now all this leaves the economist in a very odd position. As a man and a citizen, he may be (and often is) very critical of the evaluation of ends to which, under the rule of the market, the distribution of scarce resources must conform. But in so far as he is thus critical it follows that he will at times find himself in his professional capacity engaged in displaying the exquisite subtleties of the mechanism by which we contrive most effectively to make the wrong use of our limited resources; and by "wrong," it must be remembered, is meant not merely objectionable to the observer himself, but (so far as he can judge) actually unacceptable to the very people whose wishes are theoretically sovereign. Now I do not say that it is impossible to maintain this duality between one's professional and non-professional self; but I do very seriously suggest that such a position must be an uncomfortable one, and that a study of the roads to maximum accomplishment of possibly injurious ends is a pursuit hardly likely to appeal to the keenest, still less to the most creative, types of mind. Viewed from this angle, the conduct of economic analysis certainly does not become in any way impossible: but itcannot but appear rather artificial and silly—crippled, in fact by arbitrary and stultifying limitations.

Nor do these limitations become any less irksome if we fall back upon the position, plausible enough on the face of it, that those who wish to do good must be prepared to study the workings of evil. The analogy with medical research is tempting here; but it is quite inappropriate. To be sure, nobody thinks of finding fault with doctors who devote themselves to study of the processes by which noxious bacteria, for example, accomplish their evil work within the human body. And why not? Because everybody understands that all such study is ultimately motivated by, and focussed upon, the objective of defeating or eliminating the processes in question. Of course it is not necessary that the specialist in, say, some line of cancer research should expressly remind himself every day that he is working only to conquer malignant disease. The ultimate objective, in fact, may seldom present itself to his conscious mind; and in his professional zeal he may even refer to "beautiful" cases of the most disgusting and painful maladies. But it can hardly be disputed that a great deal of the laborious and patient research into human disease now undertaken would simply lose its interest, if investigators were required to adopt a strictly neutral attitude in regard to the desirability of good health, parallel to the neutrality which the economist is asked to observe in regard to the preference-scales that govern the market.[1]

Now contrast the position of the economist. Very probably he was first attracted to the subject by a desire in some way to alleviate the lot of his fellows. Like his colleague the doctor, he hopes to "make things better." Like the doctor also, he recognizes that positive and normative must be rigidly distinguished; and accordingly he embarks upon an analysis of market processes, which he hopes will be as scientifically detached and dispassionate, and as ultimately useful, as the morbid anatomist's study of diseased

[1] If anyone doubts the reality of this connection between desired objective and scientific enquiry, let him reflect, for a moment, upon the attitude of the medical profession itself towards research into such matters as contraception, in which there is no such unanimity about the propriety of the end to be attained as there is in regard to health; and where the doctor must distinguish between his expert authority as a doctor upon questions of means, and his necessarily lay opinion, as a man, on the merits of the end. Here we have a much closer analogy to the dichotomy which causes the economist so much trouble. And in this case it will, I think, be found that only those who are in general inclined to approve the end (voluntary control of conception) ordinarily think it worth while to undertake specialist research into the means by which this end is, or might be, achieved. It is hardly an accident that, in this connection, as in so many others, the specialist is also an advocate of his own speciality.

tissues. But at this point the analogy ends. For the economist having discovered that the market works in this or that way, producing such and such social patterns must, in his professional capacity, leave the matter there. Whatever views he may have formed as to the quality of these social patterns are just his personal opinions. If he wishes to give publicity to them, he must (if he is an honest man) do so in his own time; otherwise he is guilty of cheating the University or other body which employs him to undertake *economic* studies. And, of course, the public must be warned to ascribe no special authority to whatever pronouncements he may make as the result of any unauthorized excursions into the sphere of ends. For whereas the medical research worker will from time to time pause to assess his discoveries in the light of their contribution towards the acknowledged end of good health, no parallel concept of social health exists to give coherence to the economist's studies. Admittedly, people are not agreed about what constitutes social health in a community to the extent that they are agreed about physical health in the individual. And economic orthodoxy seeks to meet this difficulty not by inviting the economist to contribute to enquiries into the nature of social health, so that some agreement on this vital matter may perhaps be arrived at, but by an injunction forbidding him to discuss the subject at all, and requiring at all times observance of a strict neutrality in relation to ends. Thus, in the last resort, the only alternatives that offer any prospect of realizing whatever hope of "making things better" the economist may have entertained are (1) acceptance of the market norms as the criteria of social health or (2) the use in his private capacity of knowledge acquired professionally.

As we have seen, a certain number of economists solve this dilemma by choosing the first of these alternatives; but (as we have also seen) this is hardly a satisfactory position. As to the second course, this not only involves drawing the line between personal and professional in the awkward and arbitrary way already mentioned; it also, very probably, results in a great deal of the economist's professional work looking suspiciously like a waste of time. For here a further difference arises between economics and the whole range of physical sciences. Diseases, like electricity and magnetism, molecules and electrons, and all the rest of them, are (philosophical subtleties apart) things that are *there* and not man-created. If one wishes to control any of these phenomena, the only way to go about the job is to find out everything that can be learned as to their nature. The same cannot, however, be said of the market. A dispassionate enquiry into the workings of the market may certainly be interesting, fascinating even; but if the picture which it reveals is beyond a certain measure distasteful, it is reasonable to ask whether it might not be more profitable to modify, or even to abolish, the institution itself, rather than to prosecute still more detailed investigations into the minutiae of its working. The doctor, on the other hand, who seeks to control the common cold by trying to isolate the virus responsible for it, and to study the behaviour of this organism when identified, has no such alternative course to suggest. He cannot propose that we should make colds illegal, or legalize them only upon strictly limited conditions. Or, if he should be led to the conclusion that the complaint in question was of psychological origin, or was due to certain social habits or institutions, and, therefore, man-created, it would certainly not be considered trespass on his part, if he were to canvass the possibility of taking steps to abolish the disease by appropriate changes in human behaviour or social organization. Indeed, one whole branch of medicine, that connected with public health, is largely occupied with studying the connections between social institutions and health, and with propounding schemes whereby these institutions may be better adapted to prevent and cure various forms of sickness. We should regard anyone who proposed to confine medical research within the strait-jacket of a given set of institutions, as the economists are confined, as crazy.

At this point it is useful also to recall that positive economic analysis is not only frustrated by lack of any directing end or objective: it has also proved itself to be an instrument of only very moderate utility even for strictly positive investigation. The gap between theory and practice yawns lamentably widely. The economist is not merely unable to tell us what we ought to do: he is hardly in any better position to tell us what will happen, if we do do this, that or the other thing. For reasons explored at length in Chapter 2 of this essay, the practical applications of economic analysis are apt to be disappointingly unfertile, owing to factors which are inherent in the nature of the material to which this analysis is applied. And finally, we may recall that in this respect the situation looks like getting worse rather than better; since the growth both of monopolies, and (still more) of deliberate state interference with economic affairs, is rapidly depriving market processes of that objectivity which alone makes them conformable to systematic laws.

In these conditions it is difficult to resist the conclusion that the contemporary forms of economic analysis are more intimately related with a particular historical epoch than our "scientific" economists are usually willing to admit. This, of course, is one of the shapes in which the charge that the economists are just the paid sycophants of capitalism commonly appears; but it is not necessary to be a Marxist, or even to impute sinister motives to the economists, in order to detect a connection between their theories and their historical environment. Indeed, if they were not sensitive to, and if their work was not conditioned by, this environment, they would lay themselves wide open to the charge of indifference to reality—of apple-pie fantasy-weaving, in fact. In the nineteenth century, market economics, at least on the positive side, was no doubt reasonably close to actualities. For it is a commonplace that the ideal markets of economic analysis came nearer to embodiment in earthly form in the Western world of that period than probably at any other time in history. And it was just at that time that the market came to be looked upon also as an almost perfect instrument, capable of solving the perennial problem of distribution of scarce means between alternative uses, in almost every one of the myriad forms in which this presents itself. But subsequent criticism has made grave breaches in the supremacy of the market both from the positive and from the normative point of view, with the result that the economists are faced with this dilemma: either they must live in a sort of perpetual regression to the nineteenth century, like old people who are unable to let go the world of their childhood; or they must convince themselves of the wrongfulness of this criticism, and must then come into the open (in defiance of their own limitations of their own proper station) as champions of the validity of market norms. If Queen Anne is dead, enquiry into the principles governing her life on earth are of historical interest only; unless indeed one is convinced that the royal lady *both* ought to, *and* can, be resurrected.

The reader will, however, notice that up to this point I have neglected to take account of the possible fruitfulness of economic analysis in the hands of the new-style individualists. This is a very important omission; for it is perfectly possible to argue that the destruction of old-style, capitalist markets which we are now witnessing as the result of innumerable experiments in state "planning" is a transitional phase; and that out of it there could, and should, emerge a new, socialized, system of markets. Market analysis is, on this view, merely undergoing a sort of temporary eclipse. If everything goes off all right, we may hope to see it emerge to shine with brighter splendour than ever before.

In this argument there is, I think, really good and solid ground for saving *something* of the essential technique of economic analysis from the dustbin. Moreover, the case is all the stronger, in so far as there is force in the neo-individualists' plea that it is only in a socialized economy that market norms come into their own, and really deserve any serious respect as optima; and that this plea is not to be dismissed as negligible does, I think, emerge from the discussion of Chapter 5 of this essay. A socialized economy, which honestly wanted to make the market as reliable an instrument as possible for recording the social valuation of alternative products, ought to get much more accurate results than a capitalist society which simply assumes without further ado that what people can be made to pay is a proper and complete indication of what they want.

But when all this is admitted, can we be sure that intelligent and creative minds will still not be irked by the attempt to pin them down rigidly to market analysis and market analysis only, and to debar them from dabbling in ends as well as means? I doubt it. For, in the first place, even the socialist economist, who believes that the best contribution that economic theory can make to the solution of our various problems will only be realized in a socialized society, is still not strictly entitled, in his professional capacity, to put this proposition forward. For if he does so, he is once more trespassing into the sphere of ends. He is in effect saying: "Our concepts of economy are often misleading because our recorded preference-scales are often meaningless or misleading"; and this, as we have seen, is just what he must not do, since market preference-scales constitute his inviolable data.

Second, although the capacity of the market to

interpret relative preferences might be improved out of all recognition in a socialized economy, there is little prospect that it could ever become a completely reliable instrument upon whose automatic working we could implicitly rely.[1] Hence, even in the most smooth-running socialist society that the imagination can picture, it would be necessary to keep some kind of check upon the social patterns, and upon the concepts of economy that emerged from market processes; and the economist who is interested in social betterment would feel something of the same itch as he does now to scrutinize and criticize the validity of market norms in the light of external standards. In so far as the optima of the socialized markets could put up a better showing than that of the markets that we know, the itch might be less violent than it is to-day. But unless and until we reach a stage in which we are agreed that production of every kind of commodity or service should be regulated on strictly commercial principles, the itch would still be there. Or, to change the metaphor, injunctions to the economist to paddle his own canoe, and to paddle it only on the waters of the market without ever exploring where these rivers come from or where they are flowing to, would seem hardly less unreasonable than they do to-day.

And in the third place, it seems likely that the

[1] See pp. 233 ff.

student of economic analysis, who keeps loyally within the frontiers assigned to him, will find that, when this analysis comes to be applied in a socialized economy, there is little left for him to occupy himself with—at least, after a first burst of great energy. At the present time a good deal of interest is, to be sure, being displayed by trained economists of socialist views in the problems of economic analysis in a socialized economy. The subject is new, its appeal to socialists who believe that orthodox analysis has any serious significance at all is obvious, and the dazzling variety of experiments and counter-experiments in progress in the Soviet Union (and more recently to some extent also in Nazi Germany) have suddenly breathed life into his abstractions. For the time being, the economist finds more than enough hypotheses upon which to exercise his ingenuity in this field. But he would do well to remind himself that "play-competition" is after all a very different matter from the grim and complex realities of competitive profit-making in a non-socialized economy. Play-competition in a socialized economy implies the existence of socialized productive enterprises which agree to keep the rules: to keep, that is, any and every rule that the ultimate authorities—parliamentary or dictatorial—choose to lay down. Now, presumably, the responsible authorities will wish their socialized economy to work smoothly and well, and they will accordingly frame the rules of play-competition with this end in view, and especially with an eye upon the need for harmonious working in all parts of the system. To judge from contemporary theoretical discussion, this is likely to mean, in practice, that the socialized enterprises will be instructed to model themselves as closely as possible upon the pure Platonic markets of the textbooks. This, however, is almost certain greatly to reduce the range of "interesting complications." Indeed it may well be possible before long to reduce the theoretically possible changes in socialized markets to a comparatively small number of standard formulae.[1] While these formulae are being arrived at, the analytical economist will no doubt be an extremely busy and important person, and his services will be in great demand at the Ministry of Socialized Production. But once this initial stage is passed, what kind of future is in store for him?

To put the matter more concretely, a great part of the interesting (or baffling) complications of actual market processes arise from the failure of these markets to conform to textbook patterns, and from all the frictions and the lack of coordination between different parts of our economic system. In the actual

[1] Some idea of what these formulae might boil down to is given by Professor Barone's appendix to *Collectivist Economic Planning*, ed. Hayek.

economic world nobody knows, for example, where there may not be an outbreak of monopolistic action. The control of saving and investment, again, is a notoriously chancy business, quite unamenable to the discipline of orthodox market rule; and there is no end to the interesting, if disturbing, complications that arise from the failure of bankers, and of the financial world generally, to tie up their part in the distribution of scarce means between alternative uses with that of the rest of the economic system. One has only to think of the ink that has been spilled on such topics as the economic consequences of inflations and deflations, of hoarding, of over- or under-investment, to realize the part that such issues play in the daily business of the economist.

In the socialized market economy, on the other hand, where monopoly is against the rules, where every enterprise has to play the same game, and where even currency, saving and investment policies are all taken out of the hands of wayward individualists and made to conform to the prescribed pattern, the number of different theoretical possibilities that can be realized, and the consequences of which it is worth while trying to chart, will surely be very limited. Invention may change the cost of production of various products: demand may fluctuate this way and that: earthquake, fire or the mere vagaries of weather may knock the bottom out of the most careful forecasts. But all such possible contingencies are, after all, only variations of a quite limited number of standard patterns. They can all be classified as changes in the conditions of supply or of demand, and, even when allowance is made for the complicated way in which the supply of one thing is dependent upon the demand for, or supply of, another, it cannot take a *very* long time to work out all the theoretical possibilities—*in markets which can be relied upon to keep the textbook rules.* If, for example, there should be a failure of the wheat harvest in our socialized economy, all the theoretical consequences of a short supply of wheat that can possibly occur in strictly competitive textbook markets—such as increased demand for substitutes, diversion of consumption from other products, and so on—can be classified, once and for all, with at the most a week or two's work on the part of a competent analytical economist. Most of the work has in fact been done already. Complications might, indeed, still arise in the application of the analysis to concrete situations, since we should still be ignorant of such factors as the actual degree of elasticity of demand for various products at particular periods. The solution of these complications, however, would fall within the province of the tool-users, rather than that of the toolmakers:[1] of those who apply, as distinct from those

[1] See above, p. 18.

who formulate, economic principles. And even these complications would presumably be much less intricate in the socialized market economy than they are to-day, since where investor, banker, saver, entrepreneur are all effectively schooled, there remain only worker and consumer to be watched as possible sources of unaccountable and (from the point of view of theoretical orthodoxy) irregular behaviour. Whichever way one looks at the matter, it seems as if the analytical tool-makers were running a grave risk of finding themselves out of a job in our socialist society.

II

It is on such grounds as these that I cannot help thinking that the fertility and value of economic studies depends upon a ruthless disregard of present boundaries and definitions. If anything of substantial utility is to come out of the economist's work, he must be allowed to poke his nose into questions of the quality of social ends, and of the means by which these are formulated. He must retain his freedom to be as sceptical as he thinks proper about market optima, and to suggest alternative standards by which these may be checked; and (what amounts to nearly the same thing) he must bravely face the possibility that, while economical action still remains in principle identical with rational action, and is therefore a proper objective at which to aim, there is no acid test by which this objective may infallibly be distinguished in practice. Equi-marginal returns is just as good a *principle* as ever, writ large upon the heavens to guide our distribution of scarce means between this use and that; but alas! neither Providence nor the economic textbooks have provided an adequate scale by which our position in relation to this principle may be accurately measured in every imaginable situation. In the last resort, the only way to judge whether, on any given occasion, we are moving towards, or away from, this theoretical optimum will be to exercise a broad, general and possibly blundering judgment.

To many contemporary economists this attitude will, I fear, look like frankly and finally throwing up the sponge. Without a trustworthy measuring-rod, the "science" of economy, it is said, becomes meaningless: reason is indistinguishable from madness and one might as well give up straight away. Such pessimism, however, is surely a little exaggerated. It is true that all the problems of social organization would be greatly simplified if we had an infallible automatic criterion of economy; but it does not follow from this that, in the absence of such a criterion, the ordinary human faculties of judgment are completely atrophied. A few simple analogies should make this clear enough. For the problem of distributing scarce means between alternative ends already arises in many spheres into which (notwithstanding the right of entry that present definitions should give him) the economist has not yet penetrated, and in which not even the most rudimentary measuring-rod is available. Such, for example, are problems associated—to quote three random examples—with the education of a child, with the choice of a partner in marriage, or with the disposition of military forces in battle. In the education of a child there are alternative and conflicting ends to be aimed at. Independence and initiative must be weighed against readiness to submit to the necessary discipline of social living: the need to cultivate the mind must be weighed against the claims of physical welfare: and so on. Yet in this common and vital matter we have to allocate the scarce time and resources available without the aid of any automatic system of weighing the importance of the various competing ends in view. No mechanism assigns marks, as the market assigns prices, to these ends, so as to make possible precise qualitative comparison between them. Yet nobody suggests that in the absence of any such automatic mechanism, it is absolutely impossible to make any kind of distinction between a more, and a less, desirable distribution of the resources available; or that it is not worth while making a serious study of all the issues involved; or that nothing of value has been, or can be, learned by those who try to make themselves experts in education. Of course, all educational problems would be a great deal less baffling if the exact relative merits of alternative plans could be read off on an automatic scale; but the fact that this is unfortunately impossible has not driven, and should not drive, the educationalists to put up the shutters, and abandon themselves to an attitude of nihilistic despair.

So also with the other examples suggested above. A man who contemplates the choice of a wife, or a woman who has to decide between competing suitors, is faced with a strict problem in economy, as defined. The scarcity of means (in a monogamous country) is evident. Only one life can be lived, only one possible partner chosen. Somehow or other the conflicting attractions—the physical beauty of one candidate, the industry of another, the gaiety of a third—have to be balanced against one another in deference to this limitation. And again we have no mechanism for weighing the conflicting ends, no ready-reckoner by which to identify the optimum decision; and yet no one takes the view that on that account it is useless to think about the problem at all, and that one might as well plump blindfold for any one of the alternatives open! Nor, to take my third example, do we take for granted that, since the commander of an army cannot figure out balance-sheets showing in price terms the estimated results of disposing his man-power and other resources in this or that fashion, it must follow that all his guesses are blind and that there is no such thing as military art or science. And these examples could be multiplied many-fold. In both personal and social affairs it is continually necessary to weigh alternatives without any adequate instrument for evaluating them, and to perform the apparently impossible feat of measuring incommeasurables against one another. Though the lack of such an instrument makes the job immensely more difficult, even this handicap does not wholly preclude the exercise of intelligence upon it; and it is still true that a false scale is worse than no scale at all.

There is, however, another sense in which the result of permitting economists to dabble in ends, and to break through the limitations of the market, is probably equivalent to signing the death-warrant of their peculiar specialism. For, once these limitations are off, the specialist study of "economy" begins to dissolve into much more comprehensive enquiries into the nature of social welfare, based in their turn upon a wide variety of expert enquiries in a great many fields. The terms "economics" and "economist" then become something of misnomers, since, as we have seen, the mere action of economizing, irrespective of what one economizes in or for, is hardly a fruitful field of enquiry; and the economists of to-day may well find that the only alternatives open to them are either to accept their own extinction; or to reassert their title to the vague and extensive realm to which Marshall[1] long ago laid claim—to set up, in fact, as students of "mankind in the ordinary business of life," or of such "individual and social action as is most closely connected with the attainment and with the use of the material requisites of wellbeing." But the fate of the economists, as economists, must be treated as of secondary consequence. The delimitation of academic specialisms is (vested interests apart) only a matter of convenience. As knowledge grows, old boundaries and classifications become both obsolete and irksome, as experience abundantly testifies. If progress is to continue, fluidity is essential. And to the charge that concepts of social welfare or even of "the material requisites of wellbeing" are hopelessly vague and woolly, in comparison with the neatly-mapped territory of Robbinsian economics, the only answer is that nobody could expect it to be otherwise. When new ground is being broken in many fields one must expect boundaries to get messed up and specialists to encroach upon one another's territories.

[1] See above, p. 41.

III

The important thing, in fact, is not the nomenclature applied to particular branches of study, or the enforcement of a law of trespass between experts in different fields. The important thing is to know what kind of enquiries are likely to be fruitful in terms of social welfare; or (to retain the economist's phraseology) what kind of enquiries will throw light upon the problem of achieving an optimum distribution of scarce means in any given situation—it being understood that this problem includes that of formulating and evaluating the ends to be pursued, as well as exploring the possible methods of achieving these ends, when known. In short, this is the question that we now face: to what field other than the continued elaboration of economic theory ought the student who is interested in social affairs to direct his energies?

On this immense topic I can only offer a few outline sketches, in the hope that these will stimulate others to more active and precise researches of real social utility. These tentative suggestions fall into five main groups, namely: (1) realistic applications of existing economic analysis within the imperfect market economy of contemporary experience; (2) studies of existing social situations and trends; (3) enquiries into the nature of social ends in modern communities, and the means of formulating these; (4) research into the technical problems connected with the satisfaction of social ends; and (5) attempted formulation of plans of social betterment. A few words are said below about each of these fields in turn. Unhappily for the contemporary economist, many of the researches indicated call for a type of training and equipment quite different from that with which he is ordinarily provided. But this, which is his private misfortune, cannot be allowed to divert attention away from quarters in which it seems likely that the most socially useful results may be obtained.

First, then, comes the task of applying existing economic analysis to the actual markets of the contemporary economic world. This job is already being done, and done by professional economists, though not, of course, by those whose primary interest lies in the sphere of analysis. The kind of thing that I have in mind here is illustrated by attempts to give spatial and temporal content to such concepts of theory as elasticity of demand, increasing returns, law of substitution and, in fact, all the ghostly theoretical terms of the tool-makers. To give an idea of the ghostliness of these ghosts, I will quote one or two short extracts from theoretical economic studies, indicating the points at which hypotheses or abstractions occur, which, if the analysis is eventually to serve as a key to practical affairs, will have somehow to be clothed with the flesh and blood of actual example in concrete reality. The first is from Professor J. H. Jones's *Economics of Private Enterprise*,[1] and reads as follows (the words within square brackets are my own notes of the points at which, sooner or later, there will have to be reference back to experience): "Given a certain elasticity of demand the supply which the monopolist will produce (and, therefore, the monopoly price) will depend upon the conditions of production." [What are actual elasticities of demand and what supply do monopolists actually produce in alternative actual conditions of production?] "If the law of diminishing returns is in operation the supply will be less (and therefore, the price will be higher) than it would be if the law of increasing returns were in operation." [Where and when do the laws of increasing or diminishing returns respectively operate and what are the realized effects in each case upon supply?] ". . . The exact arithmetical result varies according to the degree of elasticity of demand and the strength with which the law of diminishing (or increasing) returns operates." To this passage, Professor Jones rather hopefully adds the statement that "The reader will be able to supply illustrations for himself." In a general way, the reader no doubt will be able to do so; but this is not enough. For nothing of practical value has been accomplished until, not only has the reader himself supplied occasional hypothetical illustrations

[1] P. 255.

of the general principles enunciated, but the actual occurrence of the various hypotheses enunciated has also been identified in practical experience, and their relative frequency and importance evaluated.

A second example is taken from a work in which theory is in many respects unusually closely linked up with practical application—Mr. Keynes's *General Theory of Employment, Interest and Money.* Summarizing and restating his previous arguments, Mr. Keynes writes:[1] "An increment (or decrement) of employment is liable, however, to raise (or lower) the schedule of liquidity-preference; there being three ways in which it will tend to increase the demand for money, inasmuch as the value of output will rise when employment increases, even if the wage-unit and prices (in terms of the wage-unit) are unchanged, but in addition, the wage-unit itself will tend to rise as employment improves, and the increase in output will be accompanied by a rise of prices (in terms of the wage-unit) owing to increasing cost in the short period." To link this analysis up with actualities we need to see all these processes actually in operation; to observe the value of output visibly rising as employment increases, while the wage-unit and prices (in terms of the wage-unit) remain unchanged; and to register the rise in the wage-unit that occurs as employment improves, and the rise in prices (in terms

[1] Pp. 248, 249.

of the wage-unit) that accompanies the increase of output. That the reader has already observed these phenomena for himself is, to say the least, somewhat improbable. It is, therefore, somebody's business to go into the world of experience and search for evidence that these ingenious abstractions do (or do not, of course) represent concrete realities.

To avoid compiling a wearisome list of examples, I will refer to only one other book—Professor Chamberlin's *Theory of Monopolistic Competition.* In the closing paragraph of this work the author states quite frankly "No applications to particular economic problems have been attempted, or even suggested." My own point is that Professor Chamberlin's work must remain incomplete until these applications are attempted, and that this is a more urgent task than further elaboration of theory on and from the point at which he has left it. For it is unwise to carry the building of theoretical superstructures too far, unless one is reasonably confident of the security of the foundations. There is always the danger that, for example, close contact with experience might reveal divergences in the actual behaviour of monopolistic competitors from the theoretical patterns elaborated, say, by Professor Chamberlin; and that, in consequence, from the point at which such divergence occurred the "theory of monopolistic competition" might be travelling away from, rather than towards, the goal of an accurate and comprehensive explanation of actual experience.

In this connection, the reader who has followed the argument of Chapter 2 of this essay will appreciate that, while I do most decidedly hold that the economist ought to get busy with the job of referring theory back to the test of practice, I am acutely conscious that there are severe limitations upon the value of what can be accomplished in this field. Owing to the complexity and uniqueness of economic situations, what Mr. Keynes[1] has called our "practical intuition" has largely to take the place of clear concrete demonstration; and practical intuition is a poor instrument for scientific investigation. Still, even this instrument is likely to be much more valuable if it feeds continually upon a mass of hard fact, well-digested, than if it attempts to operate in a vacuum.

I have said that this work is already being put in hand. For illustrations, I may refer again to such studies as the later chapters of Mr. Clark's *National Income and Outlay*; and to the very welcome news that the Economic Intelligence Service of the League of Nations is to test out current theories of the trade cycle (as presented in Professor Haberler's recent masterly summary[2]) by reference back to historical data. Since it is clear that some of the more practical-

[1] *General Theory of Employment, Interest and Money*, p. 249.

[2] *Prosperity and Depression*, by G. von Haberler.

minded economists are already alive to the need for thus tossing their theories over to the buffetings of experience, it is not necessary to enlarge further upon this particular aspect of the subject.

IV

My second group of projected researches was described as: studies of existing social situations and trends. This covers an immense field, and the particular list of topics which happen to be mentioned here as deserving of investigation, must be regarded as merely illustrative, and not at all as comprehensive.

In this class I should list demographic researches into the make-up of populations, rates of reproduction, migration and all the vast range of matters commonly covered by what are generally called Social Surveys. In England and Wales a number of detailed surveys have recently been made of certain geographical districts—notably London and the distressed areas. These surveys have already provided material of the greatest value for the relatively limited areas which they cover. What we want is that investigations of similar comprehensiveness should be undertaken for the whole country (ideally, of course, for the whole world), and that the results should be kept continually up-to-date. The aim in view should be to include everything that contributes to a full and accurate picture of the way in which the populations covered actually live; that is to say, of the end-results, in terms of human experience, of the particular distribution of scarce means which prevails from time to time. The picture needs to show in full detail income and class structure (including of course any emerging changes in these or other conditions); housing, health standards, occupations; forms of expenditure; and social habits.

It is perhaps also desirable to add that detailed enquiries into social conditions of this kind should not, as is commonly the case at present, deal only with what the Americans so delicately describe as the "under-privileged." Necessarily, of course, so long as things are as they are, the *bulk* of social investigation must deal with the economically less fortunate classes, for the simple reason that these constitute the overwhelming majority of any large community. But we have now a very substantial middle class, while the upper economic levels of our society, though numerically small, are both economically and socially very significant. It is important that we should be just as fully informed about the incomes, modes of living and expenditure of these groups as about those of anybody else. Where information can most easily be collected by questionnaire, or house-to-house visitation, nobody should, as now too often seems to happen, be exempt on account of social position. In the past a good deal of valuable, though as yet limited, data, has come to light as the result of analysis of sample working-class budgets. These budgets have been collected by written questionnaire, often with the aid of interested voluntary societies, or, alternatively, by direct enquiry by investigators on the doorsteps. But the scope of corresponding enquiries into the income, family structure and so on of the prosperous classes is still exceedingly scanty in comparison, nor has the same technique of enquiry been applied on anything like the same scale. In consequence, there are gaps in our knowledge of the social and economic structure, which can prove exceedingly awkward. For example, the problems connected with saving and investment have been the subject of an immense amount of hypothetical discussion, and whole theories of the trade cycle have been built upon unverified hypotheses as to the behaviour of rich persons. It has, for instance, been widely asserted (and no less widely denied) that much of the mischief of a slump arises from the existence of a class of persons who are so much embarrassed with riches that they cannot find any way of spending their incomes in full. A great deal of such discussion could, however, have been short-circuited, had direct enquiry into the facts been undertaken. The owners of large incomes are in a much better position to tell us what they do, than we are to find this out by guesswork; and they ought to be asked. And, since there are, after all, not very many of them (the number of persons with incomes of over £2,000 per annum in this country is now only about 85,000[1]), the job of investigating their behaviour should not be an impossibly large one.

In short, I should like to see a regular corps of investigators, whose business it would be to prepare, and to keep continually up to date, a picture of the social structure of the whole community. (In the lamentable absence of any firm and general grasp of the social and economic unity of the whole world, I suppose community must be interpreted to mean "country.") A (necessarily meagre) sketch of the kind of work to be done was provided some years ago by the picture of the *Social Structure of England and Wales* published by Messrs. Carr-Saunders and Jones. This work is now, naturally, out-of-date, and the job wants doing again, and on a much larger scale. Alongside of this picture, also, we need to have another, illustrating in parallel fashion, what may be called the industrial structure of the community, and including such things as the forms of industrial management, the scope of monopoly and the geographical location of industry.

Partly under Government auspices, and partly as the result of the initiative of private economists, a good deal of research of this type is actually in progress.

[1] Seventy-ninth Annual Report of the Commissioners of Inland Revenue.

There is, however, not nearly enough of it; and anyone who himself participates in it can readily point out a great number of gaps to be filled in. Moreover, realistic social and economic research has had to face very severe discouragement from some of our analytical economists; and it is most needful that those who are persuaded of its usefulness should put up a bold case on its behalf. Professor Robbins, for instance, speaks for an influential school of opinion, when he writes of "the sense almost of shame" provoked by "the incredible banalities of much of the so-called theory of production—the tedious discussions of the various forms of peasant proprietorship, factory organisation, industrial psychology, technical education, etc. which are apt to occur in even the best treatises on general theory"[1] by writers who have overstepped the scarce-means-in-alternative-uses definition, and allowed themselves to discuss *any* aspect of the production and distribution of "wealth."

Such criticism cannot just be disregarded. Where I myself think that it goes wide of the mark is in so far as (on the Robbinsian view of the proper scope of economic studies, consistently enough) it fails to appreciate the value of a great deal of realistic social research from a normative point of view. If the economist ought to confine himself solely to *explanations*, or to positive analysis, then it does indeed follow that

[1] *Nature and Significance of Economic Science*, p. 65.

disquisitions about peasant proprietorship, and so forth, are only permissible where they serve as a check upon the validity of a hypothesis which has itself been arrived at by "merely thinking."[1] But if, on the other hand, the directing aim is to see in what respect social conditions may be improved, then every institution which has potentialities of good or evil ought to be subjected to the closest scrutiny. In practice, the discussions to which Professor Robbins refers nearly always relate to institutions or activities which play a large part in the lives of some group of persons. For example, it makes a great deal of difference to a cultivator whether he owns his own land, or if not, on what terms he contracts for its use with the landlord. The social student, therefore, who allows himself to be interested in the *welfare* of cultivators and landlords is doing a useful—in fact an absolutely essential—job in informing himself as fully as possible about the various ways in which their mutual relations are, or have been, adjusted.

Such research as I am here trying to suggest should in fact bring to light two more or less clearly distinguishable categories of knowledge, both of which are in their own way equally valuable. On the one hand it will reveal certain basic conditions in our social life which it is impossible, at any rate in relatively short periods, to alter; and on the other hand it will hold up

[1] See above, p. 118.

a mirror, in which we can observe what sort of a job we are actually making of that life, within those limiting conditions. Thus, if our parents, for whatever reasons, took into their heads that they would prefer as a rule to have smaller families than those of *their* parents, nothing that we can do now can destroy the influence of *this* decision upon the size and composition of present and future populations. Research into the effects of this decision thus falls into my first category. The effective fertility, on the other hand, of those of us who have actually been born and grown to maturity is a matter which is, at least in some degree, within our own control, and which is very likely to be influenced by the kind of social environment in which we find ourselves. Investigation, therefore, into the social factors which influence this fertility may be classified under the second head.

In complex modern communities a great deal of the type of research that I am visualizing would necessarily be statistical; but not all. It would need to include also a study, in less precisely quantitative terms, of such things as our laws of property and contract—institutions which have played an immensely significant part in the shaping of all our lives. And, of course, it would be necessary to assess purely statistical information in the light of both positive theory and normative judgment; to say, in fact: "this is what is happening. So and so, or so and so, appear to be the causes of this phenomenon; this and that, or such and such, are its agreeable or its ugly features." It is indeed a curious irony that outside our own particular civilization the fetters, by which, we are told, the economists must be bound in order to prevent them from lapsing into banalities, are regarded as quite unnecessary. Anthropologists, who make the most detailed studies of communities that are culturally far removed from those of contemporary Europe or America, would be deeply, and I think legitimately, shocked to learn that their work is "tedious" and "banal" in so far as it neither serves to test theories that have been deduced from a given set of original premises, nor is referable to a precise scale of given valuations. I imagine that students of anthropology would, in general, defend their work on the ground that it is fully worth while informing ourselves about the manifold patterns of life that human societies have evolved, if only because of the light which these throw, both upon the wonderful variety of ends that man has, in different circumstances, permitted to shape his social behaviour, and upon the no less wonderful ingenuity that he has shown in devising ways of accomplishing those ends. If we are interested in making the best of things for any community anywhere, it is surely worth while ransacking *all* the available evidence as to the potentialities and limitations of the raw human stuff of which this community is composed. And surely common sense would suggest that, in this search, those fields in which we are most directly and vitally concerned (and in which, as it happens, the most detailed mass of evidence is available) should be both exhaustively and promptly searched.

I know, of course, that it is impossible completely to dispose of the objection that, since there is no accepted criterion of social health, there must remain differences of opinion as to just what enquiries are of real normative significance, and what are trivial and tedious; just as there will be differences of opinion about the scope and nature of any lessons to be drawn, or action to be taken, in the light of the picture which results from our social investigation. A detailed enquiry, for example, into the organization and structure of a particular industry—let us say local transport—may include, amongst other things, a mass of particulars about arrangement of shifts and recruitment of labour. Some will perhaps adjudge this as tedious and unimportant, while others will see in it material of significant social value, wholly relevant to a due regard for the welfare of the group employed in the industry. The whole question of how far this lack of agreed norms must restrict the scope of social research is discussed at greater length below.[1] For the moment I am only asking the reader to accept the

[1] See pp. 313 ff.

proposition that, *if* the results of research can be related to intelligent purposive action, then they cannot be dismissed as tedious and trivial. And in accepting this proposition he is not, of course, disputing that where investigations are carried out on the grand scale, some part of the results will probably turn out to be dead and useless matter. Such wastage is normal and inevitable; but better too much material than too little!

V

I turn now to my third group of enquiries: researches into the nature of social ends in modern communities and the means by which these may best be formulated. Here we must again remind ourselves that we are now blandly disregarding all the recognized boundaries of academic subjects, and simply looking in any and every specialist's department for material which may throw light upon our one overriding question, namely: how can we continually improve the use that we make of our limited means so as to get more and more satisfaction out of them? As long as we are willing to accept market valuations as universally valid, this question gives relatively little trouble, since we are, so to speak, provided with a complete classified dictionary of what to aim at. But as soon as we become at all seriously critical of either the completeness or the correctness of the market's valuations, we must accept an obligation to hunt around for the best means of supplementing its shortcomings and rectifying its errors.

Here the first step is, I think, to round up a miscellaneous body of experts, and collect from them all that they have to say about the nature, and the relative urgency, of various human needs, *as these appear to each from his own standpoint*. We may begin with needs that are in some form or other universally recognized as essential to human existence or bodily welfare—such, for example, as a suitable diet. The words nutrition, malnutrition and under-nutrition have lately crept into a prominent place in the vocabulary of persons interested in social welfare. This, I suggest, is a healthy sign, and a good example of the kind of information that such experts as the physiologists, or the bio-chemists, can contribute towards answering our basic question. Let us then enquire of these experts what sort of food people in different circumstances (of climate, occupation and the like) *ought* to want, *according to their judgment*. And let us put similar questions to the appropriate specialists in regard to other recognized needs. Let us get from them everything, for example, that they can discover about the effect on the human organism of different types of housing, or of clothing. For the moment, in fact, let us frankly regard our fellow-creatures as though they were cattle or slaves, whose health and fitness is of the greatest importance to their masters, but who are without any voice in their own destiny. And let us extend these enquiries also to the psychological or psycho-physical aspects of welfare. The psychologists and anthropologists must be invited to contribute everything that they know about the ways of living that make for psychological wellbeing within a social environment; addressing themselves, for example, to such questions as: to what extent is variety of consumption necessary for, or detrimental to, psychological welfare? How far is the need for such variety related to differences in occupation, or in innate psychological traits? What is the psychological effect of alternative ways of occupying leisure time? How do people react to life in communities of varying size, or to urban, suburban or rural environments? What elements in different cultures, and what patterns of behaviour, are psychologically significant, and what secondary, and capable of modification to suit, say, new technical conditions without grave mental damage? I am, of course, here stating only the broadest questions. When these come to be tackled, they will need to be split up into much more detailed sub-heads; but I hope that even quite rough outlines will indicate both the starting-point and the objective which should govern this kind of research. The long and the short of it is that we want to know everything that anyone can tell us that may throw light upon what *would be* the optimum use of resources, on the assumption that the last word is with the expert every time.

This, however, is only the first step. Most of us do not believe that men are cattle. Most of us do not even believe that men are just more highly differentiated cattle—cattle with more complex nervous systems. Hence in the practical evaluation of social ends, some sort of balance has to be struck between what the expert thinks that we ought to want, and what we ourselves think that we do want. In arriving at this balance, it would seem that the cooperation of the psychologist, the physiologist, the biologist and the plain man is essential. Research is, in fact, called for into the value placed by ordinary people on freedom of choice in different fields. As we have seen,[1] the market economy makes quite unproven assumptions both as to the range, and as to the method, of choice likely to give the most satisfactory interpretation and evaluation of social ends. The validity of these assumptions needs to be put to independent tests, presumably on the basis of sample enquiries, as to the value that people do, in fact, set, in various circumstances, upon their liberty to flout the experts in different branches of human welfare.

In this connection, moreover, it has to be remembered that choice is not the same thing as informed

[1] See pp. 187 ff.

choice. It seems likely that there are fields in which people quite definitely wish to be relieved of choice, and are in no way psychologically damaged by evading the burden that it imposes; while in others they value highly the right to make up their own minds—but only *in the light of all available data.* The physician knows very well how these spheres melt into one another in his own field. There are occasions when all that the patient needs or wishes is to be told what to do—to devolve responsibility on "doctor's orders." In other cases, the sick man wants only to know the expert's reading of the situation, in order that he himself may make up his own mind as between, e.g. a shorter and gayer, or a longer and more invalidish, life. But it hardly seems probable that there exists any well-rooted preference for the exercise of choice upon data that are perverted or suppressed, rather than upon the basis of the most accurate information available.

Hence in some cases what now appears as a willingness to "leave it to the expert" may, in fact, only be a preference for the expert's informed, as against one's own uninformed, opinion. A homely example is afforded by the instructions often enclosed with various proprietary products in common use, let us say, some cleaning material. An instruction that reads "Articles cleaned with this preparation must not be dried in sunlight" will probably be implicitly obeyed.

inasmuch as the consumer does not know whether the effect of the sun will be, e.g. to set the stuff on fire, to damage its colour or texture, or merely to render the cleansing less effective. If, however, he knew that it was only the last-named result that was to be expected, it is quite possible that there would be times when the advantage of quick-drying would outweigh the disadvantage of an imperfect result, and he would appreciate freedom to make his own informed decision.

The relevance of these somewhat platitudinous observations to the problem of formulating social ends lies in the need to investigate ways and means of making consumer-choice better informed. The ballot of the market-place does not tell us everything; but it does tell something, and I have argued that its voice might, in certain conditions, be much more worth listening to than is generally now the case. One of these conditions is that the voters should be well supplied with accurate and relevant, and not misled by false, data about the products that are submitted to their judgment. On this topic it would be very useful, first, to know more of what happens at present (what in particular is the effect of modern advertising methods?) and, second, to explore methods by which the public might be put wise both about what is offered to them for sale, and about what the experts think that they ought to purchase.

In the light of such enquiries it should be possible

to form rough ideas as to the limits within which the market may be trusted in the interpretation of social ends. This leaves us with the problem of what to do about those ends which cannot be handled by this means. And here we are brought up sharply against one of the most complex issues which face modern societies—and one, too, which it is becoming daily more difficult to evade. We have seen that, in practice, market criteria are more and more frequently overruled by the fiat of interfering governments. Up to the present, however, it seems that these governments have only formed the most rudimentary conception of the part which they might play in promoting an optimum distribution of resources. Authoritarian interference with the market, as it is to-day, may be roughly divided into two categories, according as it is undertaken by dictators, or by governments of countries in which at least the forms of political democracy are observed. Under the dictatorships, the dictators are themselves sole judges of the optimum. If they say that there should be more guns and less butter, or more constructional work and less production of consumables, their opinion automatically settles the matter; whereas in the democracies only the most meagre attempts seem as yet to have been made to visualize economic policy as a whole, or to coordinate the various restrictions placed upon market autonomy in terms of any clearly conceived common objective.

The only general rule appears to be to give in weakly to whatever vested interest manages to press hardest.

In consequence of this very brief (and quite inconclusive) experience, a fairly widespread belief has grown up that what is called "planning" is incompatible with political freedom; and that on this account lovers of democracy are entitled to dismiss the whole subject of planning without more ado. This view commonly carries a quite illegitimate implication that the pattern of production is at present democratically determined;[1] but even apart from this, the evidence in support of it is of the flimsiest. Those who are critical of the infallibility of the market will, however, mark down the relation between economic planning and political freedom as a subject that most urgently calls for investigation. Starting from the two propositions (1) that the optimum to be aimed at must be optimum in terms of common welfare and (2) that the ballot of the market-place is an imperfect guide to this goal, we need to examine any possible additional channels through which the common man's conception of the common welfare might find expression. There are already a few first experiments afoot. The British Broadcasting Corporation, for example, does not sell its products upon market principles; but it is at great pains to try and find out what the public think about the results. The machinery that is employed for this

[1] See my *Plan or No Plan*, p. 309.

purpose would be worth looking into. Again, the Russian invention of "self-criticism" represents, though within a strictly limited field, an attempt to get a running popular commentary upon day-to-day economic policy. It is true that the existence of "reserved subjects," too sacred to be blown upon by any breath of criticism, has seriously narrowed the possibilities of this method as applied in the Soviet Union; but it does not follow from this that there may not be much to be learnt, even from this restricted experiment. And, to come right home to our own familiar world, it is, I believe, increasingly the practice of business firms to seek to elicit the opinions and criticisms of their customers by more direct and complex methods than mere inference from figures of sales. All these are rudimentary examples of attempts to get the public to express their judgments of the distribution of scarce means otherwise than through the machinery of the market; and from this point of view the methods, achievements, potentialities and shortcomings of such experiments would be well worth examination.

In short, there is a task here which calls for the joint activities of at least the students of politics and the psychologists. That task is to study, from a constructive angle, the formation and expression of public opinion—more particularly with an eye upon this very problem of democratic planning, that is to say, of getting the public to supplement and correct market data by more direct expression of opinion about the proper way to distribute our scarce means. As I have already suggested,[1] it is quite possible that we should get a much clearer idea of the optimum if, instead of concentrating attention solely upon the atomized voting of the market-place, we were at pains to elicit public expressions of opinion on the *general pattern* of social life that is likely to result from alternative methods of distributing resources; and if we were also to try to find ways and means, however rough and ready, of recording popular estimation of those social ends which the market is inherently incapable of handling. Of course planning is incompatible with democracy, if it is taken for granted that the planners are not democratically-minded—taken for granted, that is to say, that those who are responsible for directing the distribution of resources do not feel the need to consult anybody but themselves in arriving at their interpretations of the optimum. But this is a ridiculous assumption; and a very paltry reason for abandoning as insoluble the problem of giving the public a voice in planning, where the planners are willing and anxious to listen.

Already, I believe, a certain amount of research has been undertaken into the methods by which public opinion may be led, misled or expressed. The advertisers and the demagogues (as distinct from the demo-

[1] See p. 188.

crats) know a good deal about the first two of these processes; but this knowledge is mostly empirical and needs to be re-examined and classified, so as to bring out what may be of constructive value in it. In this connection I should like to see attempts made, in the first place, to analyse the origins of a number of popular beliefs (well- or ill-informed) and of changes in fashion or social habits, as well as of the methods by which these have been brought about. By what means, for example, have large sections of the public been induced, within a comparatively short period, to adopt such practices as cleaning their teeth, or "hiking" on Sundays, or persecuting the Jews? How has it come to be no longer good manners to refer to the "lower classes" (and one might almost add the "upper classes" also)? Exactly how have such beliefs as that nationalization of the banks would diminish unemployment, or that Fascism is the final stage of capitalism, been implanted in those who hold them? It would be useful to trace back accurately, on the one hand, the first public appearance of these customs and opinions; and, on the other hand, the exact channels through which they have spread.

Second, we need parallel studies of propaganda that has failed. Superficial observation of the success of modern publicity methods has led to a good deal of cynicism as to the gullibility of the public, carrying very pessimistic implications as to the prospects of any intelligent democratic control over our common social life. I suspect, however, that this is largely due to the fact that students of these matters have concentrated their attention almost exclusively upon the successes, to the neglect of the failures, of our propagandists. Careful research into the case-history of press and other "stunts" that have fallen flat should be illuminating.

Third, it is obviously not enough for our purpose to find out the limits within which the many can be made to think and act as the few would like them to do. For constructive purposes, the opposite process of getting ideas transplanted from the heads of the many into those of the few is even more important. On this matter, there is, it is true, a scarcity of instructive material available; since most of our democrats, when they get into positions of responsibility, do not take their democracy very seriously, but conceive it to be their duty to give, much more than to take, a lead. It would, however, be quite unrealistic to suggest that the great territory covered by the experience both of political democracies and of voluntary societies has nothing to offer which could throw light upon the possibilities of reflecting, as opposed to distorting, the opinion of the many for the guidance of the few. At least that territory ought to be ransacked for whatever it may contain.

I have enlarged a little upon this question of the

relations of planning and democracy because it seems to me to be of crucial importance for all who wish to see human affairs managed by the intelligent co-operation of the people concerned in them. The facile conclusion that the only alternatives open to us are either blind adherence to the necessarily distorted and imperfect readings of objective markets, or slavish obedience to the fancies of a dictator, is not to be accepted without evidence. Indeed there are few lines of enquiry more urgently needed to-day than critical investigation into the grounds upon which this conclusion rests.

Finally, there remains one other line of enquiry which calls for mention under the present head. Concepts of the optimum that cannot be recorded in objective market experience have not only to be expressed and forwarded to the proper quarter; they have also to be carried into effect. In this connection it might be worth while looking at the possibilities of the market from another point of view—not as an objective process that goes its own way, but as an instrument that can be deliberately employed to carry out subjective purposes. Concretely, this means that there are a number of ways in which a desired arrangement or re-arrangement of resources may be brought about—as by authoritative command, or by persuasion or by inducement. One may say "Work this mine or you go to jail," or "work this mine and you will be doing a public service"; or one may fix the price of coal at a figure which makes working the mine look a very attractive proposition. The third method illustrates what I mean by the expression "using the market as the instrument of subjective purposes." The experience of the Soviet Union would be well worth detailed scrutiny from this point of view; for there is no doubt that the elaborate apparatus of prices and markets in use there, while externally so closely resembling that of, say, our own country, has actually been deprived of a great part of its objectivity.[1] And here at last is a job in which the specialized training of the economist would be an asset!

VI

My fourth group of investigations, described above as research into the technical problems connected with the satisfaction of social ends, is strictly complementary to that just mentioned. For one wants to know not only what to aim at, but also, and equally, what are the possibilities of achieving the aims chosen. Under this head, accordingly, there fall, in the first place, technical researches, as ordinarily so-called, into materials, processes and so forth. These are neces-

[1] For examples of valuable work already begun in this field, see Hubbard, *Soviet Money and Finance*, and Reddaway, *The Russian Financial System*.

sarily the business of the appropriate expert. Botanists or biologists, for example, can contribute such data as the number of days' sunshine necessary to ripen different varieties of wheat, or the effect of artificial light upon the fecundity of hens; geographers can be asked to list the quantity and location of the resources with which this planet is endowed; while physicists and chemists can get to work to explore the possibilities of building our houses of bakelite or glass, or our roadways of rubber, or of taking the hangover out of alcohol.

In the second place, this field of enquiry must cover what may be called the human aspects of production. The actual business of effecting any given distribution of scarce means is only accomplished by the labour of men and women. Technical equipment and raw materials are alike dead stuff until brought to life by human effort; and it is thus the peculiarity of the human element in economic affairs that it stands, as it were, on both sides of the account—first as the source of the great complex of wants which production exists to satisfy, and second as the instrument through which this satisfaction is actually achieved. Consequently the intelligent disposal of scarce means is as much a matter of wise utilization of man-power as of any other "factor of production"; and it is essential to enlarge our understanding of the nature of this human stuff, and the conditions under which it does its best.

Here we certainly have plenty to learn. The industrial and vocational psychologists have blazed a trial along which a very substantial army of investigators might advantageously march. We want, for example, a much fuller knowledge of the actual human material available, classified according to its capabilities, aptitudes and interests. At present we have a number of isolated studies, based on intelligence-testing and the enquiries of vocational guidance experts; but these cover only a very small part of the field, and practically no attempt has been made to correlate them with the other side of the picture—with the demands, that is to say, of our economic organization. We have marked down a few round pegs here and there, and perhaps even attempted to keep them out of square holes; but we have hardly made a serious beginning, even, of the job of thorough classification of all the great mass of pegs, let alone of comparing the results with a chart of the holes that are available for them. It is still true to say that the qualities and capabilities of the vast majority of the human race are an almost entirely unknown quantity; and it is still true to say very nearly the same of the vast majority even of English men and women. Though it must be admitted that the technique of investigation in this field is as yet rather primitive, we are still much too far from making even the fullest possible use of such tools as we have. In concrete terms, we want a survey which shows the distribution of aptitudes for different forms of manual and mental skills, and we want this correlated with pictures, both of the demands for these in industry, and of the available opportunities for their development by appropriate educational facilities. Admittedly these pictures would be sketchy and contain large blank patches; but the argument that inability to do everything is good ground for not attempting anything usually smacks of what the psychologists call "rationalization."[1]

Further, our whole attitude towards labour problems—using that term in the widest possible sense—is due for overhaul. In the past twenty years or so—and still more in the past two centuries—we have effected enormous revolutions in our working habits and methods; and, on the whole, it is true to say that these revolutions have been the outcome of technical invention in the narrow, non-human sense, and have been brought about with hardly any regard to their effect upon the human material which has, willy-nilly, to cooperate in their working. Thus, on the one hand, we have experienced changes in our social habits as fundamental as the introduction of a sharp regular daily division between work and play—a condition that must have been virtually unknown throughout

[1] If anyone doubts what can be done in this field, he would do well to study the valuable pioneering work accomplished in Mr. J. L. Gray's study, *The Nation's Intelligence*.

the long ages of pre-factory history; and, on the other hand, we see the increasing monotonization of work, its increasing speed, and (what is probably even more important) the use of devices such as the conveyor-belt which deprive the worker of all control over the pace of his own work. Without question, these things have had very significant effects upon the minds and bodies of the people who directly experience them. The technical efficiency of many of these devices is almost certainly more apparent than real, since even the lay eye can detect a compensating damage to the human factor in production; but our knowledge both of this aspect of the matter, and of the extent to which modern productive methods are really compatible with the principle of using resources in the way that gives optimum satisfaction, is very limited. There have, it is true, been a certain number of investigations by the industrial psychologists, which embody valuable material; but, as a rule, these have been restricted by an unduly narrow conception of efficiency—by the practice, that is to say, of concentrating attention upon the effects of changes in working conditions upon immediate output. We want more studies in this field, and we want them related to a broader conception of human welfare.

In this connection also, it would be useful to review the mass of conventions and uncriticized assumptions that underlie our opinions on the subject of work generally. The prevailing theories about incentives are, for example, very crude. It is variously asserted that we work from love of gain, from force of habit, from fear of starvation. Here some precise observation of actual behaviour—perhaps as much the behaviour of those who are relieved of the necessity of undertaking regular work, as of those who do not find themselves in this position—would be helpful. Scattered about the world, notably in the Soviet Union, in Germany and in the United States a good many experiments are being carried out—if somewhat half-heartedly—in the introduction of new incentives. In these there are elements of compulsion, of appeal to the sense of social obligation, of competition (not always of a strictly economic kind) and of reward by publicity instead of money. What is the view of those who have been concerned in such experiments as to what is to be learnt from them? And if (as is unhappily only too probable) many of those best qualified to speak on this matter are compelled for political reasons to remain dumb, how can their experience be repeated and extended in circumstances more favourable to disinterested enquiry?

Closely allied to such investigations also should run enquiries into what is sometimes called administrative technique. The substitution, in any field, of conscious control of policy for the automatic rule of the market immediately implies that people have to be dealt with as people, not as interchangeable units guaranteed infallibly to make the appropriate response to a given stimulus. The art of managing people as people in some common undertaking is the art of administration. Here there is a wealth of experience accumulated by governments, by large business concerns and by voluntary societies. This experience needs to be reviewed for what it can contribute to the answers to such questions as: What are the conditions that make authority tolerable? What is the scope and intensity of the rank-and-file worker's desire to share in the control of the enterprise in which he is engaged? What methods are used (and what has been their measure of success in different conditions) to regulate recruiting or promotion, to distribute responsibility or to fight stagnation? In this context the work undertaken by Institutes of Public Administration and similar bodies suggests valuable possibilities.

VII

It must, I am afraid, by this time appear that the domain of the economist has been pretty effectively partitioned among the various groups of technicians, and that the outlook for his future is in the highest degree dismal; for practically all the researches proposed under the two preceding headings are highly technical; and what has been aptly termed "amateur technology"[1] is obviously an indefensible nuisance, of which, for very shame, our economist would hardly wish to be guilty. It remains only to ask whether this is indeed the end of the matter, or whether there is still some useful part to be played that is within even the economist's competence.

If by "economist" is meant a professional student of the practice of economizing, that is to say of distributing scarce means between *given* alternative ends, it will by now be plain enough that, for my own part, I am unable to hold out any great hopes for the future. But if the term is stretched to permit of discussion of ends as well as of means, and "economist" is redefined, however loosely and vaguely, as "student of social welfare," then I do not think that the last word has yet been said. For, quite apart from the researches comprised under my first two heads that is to say, enquiries on the one hand into the applications of current economic theory to existing market economies, and on the other hand into social situations and trends, most of which are well within the competence of many contemporary economists—quite apart from all these, the last word is never with the technicians. In the last resort, the results of technical research have to be woven into a pattern of social welfare. This means that our social student may still have a part to play in indicating in what directions technical research

[1] Robbins, *Nature and Significance of Economic Science*, p. 42.

is most urgently called for. For he will necessarily observe that our distribution of scarce means looks less satisfactory at some points than at others. And it will be just to these critical points that he will call the attention of the technicians. For example, it may well be thought that the manner in which we in England distribute our resources produces an excessive urbanization. Those who think so will naturally wish the appropriate experts to look into the possibilities of rural development; to see whether, for instance, there is anything in the idea that, in this electrical age, industry might go back again to the countryside from which it was expelled by the exploitation of steam-power; or whether the cultivation of, say, soya beans on British soil might not be a useful way of extending and diversifying our agriculture. In this indeed there is in principle nothing new; nor is it in any way derogatory to the prestige of the technicians to suggest that their researches should be linked up with, or even guided by, considerations that lie outside their own peculiar province. Already, in the market economy, technical research of all kinds—whether concerned with processes or products or the search for materials—is intimately bound up with the market's own valuations. The technicians are frequently employees of the entrepreneurs, just as much as are any other grade of workers, and they are employed for the express purpose of contributing to the more effective and economical satisfaction of market demands. Their researches are not conducted in a vacuum, but arise from, and are intimately related to, this particular context. If the rule of the market is to be tempered by concepts of social welfare hitherto neglected, this will mean a corresponding re-alignment of the activities of the technicians; and the nature of that re-alignment can only be made known by those who are responsible for interpreting, and for formulating these extra-market concepts.

What it comes to, in short, is that in any society it must be somebody's business to correlate the disconnected activities of the technicians; to acquaint himself with the results of their work and, in the last resort, to choose between the alternative possibilities that these open up. In so far as this choice is not left to be determined by the automatic mechanism of the market, it is supremely important that it should be made with the most wide-open intelligence possible. As I have said more than once, the fact that a thing is not left to decide itself, or cannot be read off an automatic scale, does not imply that it must be dismissed with a shrug of the shoulders. If, in either our individual, or our social, lives, we had habitually behaved like children who only tackle those sums to which precise answers are provided at the end of the book, we should hardly have climbed even as far as we have up the path of civilization. Every day we are making choices in cases where the data are grievously inadequate, and where we cannot *know*, even after the event, whether one of the rejected alternatives might not have been preferable; and yet most of us, most of the time, are convinced that these choices come out better when we use the best of our intelligence upon such data as are available, than when we adopt an attitude of impotent despair.

There is need, therefore, of a continuous stream of informed criticism directed upon the pattern that results from whatever distribution of scarce means actually prevails from time to time; so that whatever modifications are made in that pattern (and in a vigorous community it should be in a state of continuous change) should be made as intelligently as possible. It may, of course, be argued that, at least in a democratic society, such criticism is not a specialist's job at all; that it is the layman's business to chew over the data supplied by all the various experts and then to decide what is to be done; and that there is indeed something repugnant in the idea of a group of students setting up to be experts in social welfare. Such decisions, it may be said, as, for example, whether in a particular district resources should be diverted from the building of schools to slum clearance, or whether bread should be supplied like water out of the rates, are matters in which it is essential, if democracy is to have any real meaning, to get the fullest possible public cooperation. All this may be admitted; but it still remains true that there is a big job to be done in the coordination and presentation of all the available data to the ultimate public with whom the final decision rests. Somebody has to know about the possible types of schools that can be built, the probable number of children to be educated in the district in question, the degree of overcrowding, the facilities for re-housing the population that will be displaced through slum clearance and so on. Somebody has to form an estimate of the probable effect on the consumption of bread should it be supplied without direct payment, and the relation of this estimate to the quality and adequacy of the diet of those who will be affected by the proposed change. The architects, school teachers, builders and bakers are not, by themselves, able to contribute all that is wanted. It may be that those who make it their business to coordinate and publicize the data supplied by the technicians, and to relate these to concepts of social welfare, can only put forward very modest claims to rank as experts themselves. But it is quite certain that in all communities where passion, prejudice or sheer despair have not destroyed the conviction that by taking thought we can increase our comfort and happiness, these inexpert experts have a rôle of importance to play.

This is more or less equivalent to saying that the instinct of those who coined the term "political economy" was a sound one: that of those who scrapped this in favour of "economics" or "economic science" much less healthy. And the use of the older nomenclature would also be more appropriate to the last of the heads into which the jobs that await the economist or his coadjutors were divided above, viz. the attempted formulation of plans of social betterment.

This heading, the meaning of which it is now time to amplify, should perhaps be regarded less as descriptive of a separate line of enquiry, than as an angle from which all our other projected researches should be approached. For those who believe that social studies ought always to be informed with the purpose of social betterment cannot afford to let this aspect of their work slide out of view for long at a time. And this is equally true whether they are discussing relatively detailed sections of the field, such, for instance, as the distribution of intelligence among the inhabitants of a particular parish, or the incidence of unemployment in a decaying coal-field; or whether they are interested in such broad issues as the trade relations between the members of the British Empire, or intercontinental migrations. In every case, the intelligent enquirer is quite certain to come upon conditions of which he is disposed to be critical. And in so far as he does so, it is, I suggest, essential to the fertility of his work that he should both make his criticism explicit, and sketch, however roughly and provisionally the measures which he himself, in the light of his own standards of value and his own present knowledge, thinks would help to meet these criticisms. He must feel that his responsibility has not been fully discharged, if he has not made some attempt, even of the most tentative character, expressly to relate his work to the overriding objective of all humanistic studies—namely, amelioration of the conditions of human life.

In practice I do not think that this responsibility is universally accepted by students of social affairs. To those who have not evaded it, we do indeed owe most of the progress upon which we can legitimately congratulate ourselves. The realistic and constructive students of, say, unemployment, or maternal mortality, or destitution, have made invaluable contributions towards the success of attacks upon these evils; but the full potentialities of their work have only been realized in so far as they have, in the last resort, relinquished their academic detachment, and said what, in their judgment, *ought to be done*. And their example is by no means universally copied, or even respected. There are still too many workers in the field of social studies who are content with far too radical a divorce of diagnosis from prescription.

The reason for this—as I believe fundamentally unhealthy—state of affairs is, I think, to be sought in one or other of three conditions. The first is ignorance.

In many cases we give up at the stage of diagnosis, for the simple reason that we just do not know what to suggest. With this attitude one cannot but have every sympathy. The investigator, for example, who makes a study of poverty on the Tyneside, or of the struggle for existence in Japan, may well be pardoned if he finds himself wholly baffled. He can see plainly enough what has gone wrong, but may well be at a loss to suggest how this may be put right, at least without compensating damage being done elsewhere. Here, then, we have one reason for those masterly analyses, the very comprehensiveness and lucidity of which seem to serve only as aggravations of a sense of helpless despair. Ignorance, however, is a comparatively simple obstacle to deal with. If one hunts around enough, and tries hard enough, one can practically always find some plan that will ameliorate any situation, however complex or desperate. The remedy for ignorance is more, and more vigorous, search for illuminating knowledge.

A second, and more serious, obstacle to the effectiveness of social research is presented by a deeply-rooted element in our academic tradition. Students and research workers are bred in academic institutions and—as a rule at a relatively early age—their outlook becomes coloured by the traditions which prevail there. Now in the Universities of Western Europe and to some (though less) extent also in America, the ideology of teaching in the arts subjects, including social studies, is derived in the direct line from fifth-century Athens. The genealogy reads: Socrates—Renaissance—Oxford and Cambridge.

Now this Socratic influence has, I suggest, long since outlived whatever usefulness it may have originally enjoyed, and has indeed become quite seriously mischievous. It is essentially a sceptical tradition, and carries with it also the ancient Greek prejudice against any kind of knowledge that could possibly turn out to have any practical usefulness. Socrates went about Athens asking, but not answering, questions, a practice which the Athenians found so tiresome and disturbing that they put him to death. But the ultimate result of their attempt to be rid of him has only been that his spirit has been reincarnated many centuries later in academic cloisters where its survival value has been much strengthened. And, more recently, this spirit has penetrated also—and with quite disastrous consequences—into the relatively unexplored, and potentially invaluable, field of adult education. Only the natural sciences have had the good fortune to be late enough in stealing their way into our academic curricula to escape its baneful influence.

The valuable things in this tradition are the challenge which it offers to authority and the encouragement which it gives to independence of thought: qualities not to be under-estimated in this age of political dogmatism. But it is a great mistake to suppose that these cannot be separated from the sterilizing influence which Socratic scepticism has exercised upon constructive thinking. The entirely proper desire to steer clear of authoritarianism, and of biassed presentation of controversial issues has been made the pretext for a great deal of sheer irresponsibility. In our academic institutions we have now professors of international affairs, of industrial relations and of other equally practical issues. Urgent social problems are discussed in our lecture halls, where their history and complexity is often demonstrated with the greatest ability. It is, however, still entirely contrary to academic tradition that those who analyse the problems of social life should feel any obligation whatever themselves to suggest solutions. If solutions are discussed at all, it is, in my experience, as often as not merely in order to indicate the possible weaknesses of each alternative; and the teacher is content to finish his exposition, explicitly or implicitly, with some such statement as this: "I have now tried to put before you the various elements involved in the critical situation in . . . and the lines upon which this may be expected to develop. It is not any part of my business to suggest remedies, but I hope that this analysis will be useful to those of you who appreciate the gravity of the situation."[1]

[1] I should like to be able to claim that my own record was more innocent in this matter than, alas! I now see it to have been.

The effect of this kind of thing is too often to produce a sort of despairing nihilism on the part of students whose original interest in social problems may have been of an entirely constructive nature. I have myself repeatedly observed this process of degeneration actually at work, and listened to the lamentations of its victims. The more the student learns, the less he feels able to do. It is good, of course, that he should appreciate the complexity of most social problems and be critical of quack remedies; but this is only the first half of a dual process of which the second part should be definitely constructive. Imagine the beneficial revolution that would be brought about, should the principle become recognized that a writer or lecturer on social subjects had failed in his professional duty, if, when referring to problems and difficulties he did not also append constructive suggestions! And if it were equally an accepted rule that those who, in their turn, criticized these suggestions, were themselves under obligation to indicate what alternatives they would regard as preferable. As long as there is free discussion and counter-discussion, there is absolutely nothing in this procedure that could possibly be charged with dogmatism or bias; but the result of the establishment of such a code might well be that, in place of the paralysis which seems to be almost endemic among the intellectuals of our time, we should see a generation of students growing up who believed both in themselves and in the possibilities of their work.

VIII

Finally, there remains yet one more obstacle to be negotiated, if the constructive possibilities of social research are to be fully realized. This may be stated as follows: unless there is common agreement, in the broadest general terms, as to the aims of policy, the formulation of programmes becomes meaningless, if not impossible; and research must lack the coherence which is necessary to make it fruitful. Now this, it should also be observed, is a difficulty which can only arise in such communities as profess to respect the principles of democracy. Where there is a dictatorship, the ultimate aims of social policy are decided by the dictator and there is no more to be said. Research is relevant and coherent in so far as it contributes towards the attainment of whatever objectives have received the dictator's endorsement.

In a democratic community on the other hand, things may not be so simple. In the last resort the only guiding principles of a democratic society are that every member counts for one and not more than one, and that, where incompatible ends are desired, minorities must give way to majorities. So long as these principles enjoy more than nominal acceptance by the whole community the path is still reasonably smooth; for it is unlikely that, in these circumstances, there will be serious confusion about the ends of policy, or, what is nearly the same thing, about the vital matter of the difference between social betterment and social deterioration. Where, however, democracy is only skin-deep, there is a real danger that the duty of formulating programmes of social betterment, which we have laid upon the social student, may become impossible because people are not agreed upon what betterment is.

The point will be more easily appreciated if I put it in terms of a concrete illustration. England is a nominally democratic country. Programmes of social betterment for England should, therefore, rest upon the ultimate principle that every citizen counts for one, and not more than one, and that the wish of the majority must prevail over that of a minority. England is also a country where there are great differences in wealth and social privilege. Now, again on the principle that each citizen should count for one, and not more than one, it would seem that the reduction of these inequalities should be included in the aims of social policy—that our accepted standards of welfare would be more nearly realized if there were less inequality. For our system of privilege certainly enables a minority of citizens each to count, in terms of social prestige (not to mention material welfare) for very much more than one. The reduction of privilege may, of course, be a difficult objective to obtain. Social equality may involve all kinds of re-adjustments and dislocation that are far from easy to overcome; but that is not the point. On strictly democratic principles, there can be no excuse for not including social equality among the objectives which it is our business to *try* to attain, even if we have eventually to give the job up as too difficult.

In practice, however, the pursuit of social equality enjoys no such recognized status in this country, as one of the accepted ends of policy towards the achievement of which research should be directed. This will immediately become clear if we contrast the attitude of the economists (and the public) towards social equality with their attitude towards ends that do enjoy general approval—often to a degree which makes it unnecessary even explicitly to formulate them. The trade cycle is a good example here. The view that trade depressions are noxious phenomena is practically universal; and just because of this agreement, economists have spent an immense amount both of realistic research and of deductive analysis on trying to arrive at a better understanding of the nature and causation of these recurring slumps. (Even those economists who are most anxious to keep clear of normative studies seldom escape the infection; for their interest gets directed to the same quarter as the rest, and ultimately for the same reason, namely, that the trade cycle is a nuisance and that we want to be rid of it.) Now nobody questions the propriety of these enquiries (though there may be differences of opinion about which of them opens up the most fruitful line to follow), because everybody is completely of one mind as to the objective in view. This agreement, as has just been said, does not even need explicit expression. If we could find a way of controlling trade cycles, nobody doubts that we should have made a step forwards, and not backwards.

So also, in the case where a community is engaged in a great war, the prosecution of the contest provides an overriding objective to govern the direction of research. In so far as the war is publicly approved (and we may presume for the sake of argument that criticism is negligible and that what there is of it is effectively suppressed), there is no need to bother about differences of opinion about the ultimate policy to which research must be related. Every worker in every field, in these circumstances, knows the questions that he is desired to answer, and the aims which he is expected to help to promote. He "does his bit," unperturbed by any doubts as to the nature of the whole towards which these bits contribute.

But with equality it is quite otherwise. Anyone who undertook research which he hoped would facilitate the reduction of privileges of birth, wealth and social status in the expectation that this also is included in the universally accepted objectives of social policy would certainly suffer a rude shock. For there is here an open and serious division of opinion as to the very nature of social betterment. The mere fact that the desirability of social equality is often the subject of public discussion is evidence of this. Nobody bothers to debate the pros and cons of the elimination of the trade cycle because it would be a waste of time. But social equality is another matter.

In short, this matter of the public attitude towards equalitarian proposals illustrates a latent disharmony which, I believe, has had, and still has, a very grave influence in crippling the effectiveness of social research in nominally democratic communities, and indeed in paralysing their capacity for effective action of many kinds. In England it is very doubtful if the rich and privileged whole-heartedly accept the democratic principle that everybody counts ultimately for one, and not more than one. It is not, I think, much of an exaggeration to say that the comfortable classes as a whole have not yet realized that the economically unprivileged are members of the same species as themselves. Any close observer of what happens when the representatives of two groups are brought into close personal contact cannot fail at times to be struck by this. Subtle differences in the niceties of behaviour, especially those which imply personal respect, are often very revealing—most of all when they are well-intentioned. Not so long ago I heard one of our relatively prosperous citizens ask an unemployed woman, with whom he happened to have been brought into a passing business contact, to turn out her handbag in his presence—for the kindly reason that he was sincerely distressed by the thought that she might not have enough money to pay her fare to her home; but this gentleman was most resentful at the suggestion that it would be no greater discourtesy for his own wife to be asked to exhibit the contents of her purse to a stranger. Such an example could be multiplied a thousandfold by anybody who has much contact with both ends of the social scale. There must indeed be many who have asked themselves how many members of our economically fortunate groups have ever realized that, for working-class youngsters of fourteen to work long hours as errand boys carrying loads that are too heavy for them, is exactly the same thing, from the social point of view, as for their own children to be similarly employed.

Such latent disharmonies are very dangerous; for they mean that democracy often survives only in so far as there is a tacit agreement not to recognize its implications; and there is always a risk that this agreement may one day be broken. The majority may one day assert their right each to count for one, and to deny that of others to use a different arithmetic. In that event, one or other of two things must happen. Either those who have enjoyed privilege must frankly recognize the implications of their nominal acceptance of democratic principles; or the community will be disrupted, as by civil war. The implications of this situation for the future of human freedom and welfare are obviously immense; but their discussion lies outside the scope of this essay. The only points that I wish to emphasize here are, first, the fact that the democracies of to-day are apt, as in England, to be insecurely founded; second, that their survival often rests upon the observance by all classes of a "gentleman's agreement" to turn a blind eye to the full implications of their nominal creed; and third, that, inasmuch as social research depends for its fruitfulness, as I believe it invariably does, upon the prospect which it offers of accomplishing real advances in social welfare, its possibilities are cramped by the restricted interpretation which is thus placed upon this concept of welfare. When, recently, the King of the Belgians proposed the establishment of an international institute to investigate and assist in the solution of contemporary economic problems, he gave, I suspect, insufficient weight to one difficulty in the way of this admirable project—that is to the depth of the prevailing disagreement both as *to what those problems are* and *as to the actual difference between amelioration and deterioration.*

At the moment, therefore, this business of formulating programmes of social betterment and directing research towards their achievement is not by any means a simple matter. But I do not wish to end upon a note of pessimism. Ignorance is one of the easiest of all foes to combat. Academic traditions have been changed before, and may be changed again. And, as for the more serious latent disagreements as to the proper ends of social policy in our nominally democratic societies, the experience of the past is not wholly discouraging. There is always hope that those who have learnt one thing may learn another; and there is still an instructive history to be written in terms of the growth of imagination: particularly of imaginative realization of the existence of other people. The rich who, at least in England, have learned that the logic of democracy requires that the poor should have votes, may also, if we go the right way about it, come to realize that by the same logic *all* the attributes of humanity must be ascribed to *all* their fellow citizens; and then, at last, such objectives as the destruction of privilege may be pursued with all the ardour and the intellectual acumen now expended upon the fight against cancer, the trade cycle or the tsetse fly.

INDEX

Overleaf

will be found

particulars of

LONDON'S BURNING

a novel

by

BARBARA WOOTTON

BARBARA WOOTTON

LONDON'S BURNING

A NOVEL FOR THE DECLINE AND FALL OF THE LIBERAL AGE

Cr. 8vo *7s. 6d. net*

"Mrs. Wootton writes of the wrath to come. . . . She wrecks our present world for us, or rather, she pushes it a little nearer to destruction, and involves England in the catastrophe that has already overtaken several European countries, and describes for us what we are to suffer during the general strike in 1940. Mrs. Wootton is an accomplished writer and is obviously much disturbed by the present social situation. . . . Mrs. Wootton's novel is excellent in all its parts."—*Manchester Guardian*

"The author is always convincing, whether she is listening to business men gossiping over their lunch or watching an excited crowd pouring through the streets. For she possesses the essential quality for a story of this nature—a sure knowledge of the means whereby we live in modern civilization. That is why 'London's Burning' holds a warning in its wisdom. We shall disregard this Cassandra at our peril."—*Daily Herald*

LONDON: ROUTLEDGE

For Product Safety Concerns and Information please contact our EU representative GPSR@taylorandfrancis.com
Taylor & Francis Verlag GmbH, Kaufingerstraße 24, 80331 München, Germany

www.ingramcontent.com/pod-product-compliance
Lightning Source LLC
LaVergne TN
LVHW011114300926
849160LV00008B/375

* 9 7 8 0 4 1 5 6 0 8 0 0 8 *